MW00511309

Presented to

_____

By

_____

On the Occasion of

_____

Date

_____

Balance
FOR BUSY MOMS

101 Time-Management Tips

ELLYN SANNA

BARBOUR BOOKS
An Imprint of Barbour Publishing, Inc.

© 2002 by Ellyn Sanna

Cover art © PhotoDisc, Inc.

ISBN 1-58660-494-5

All Scripture quotations, unless otherwise noted, are taken from the HOLY BIBLE, NEW INTERNATIONAL VERSION®. NIV®. Copyright © 1973, 1978, 1984 by International Bible Society. Used by permission of Zondervan Publishing House. All rights reserved.

Scripture quotations marked NLT are taken from the Holy Bible, New Living Translation, copyright © 1996. Used by permission of Tyndale House Publishers, Inc., Wheaton, Illinois 60189, U.S.A. All rights reserved.

Scripture quotations marked KJV are taken from the King James Version of the Bible.

Scripture quotations marked TLB are taken from The Living Bible. Copyright © 1971. Used by permission of Tyndale House Publishers, Inc., Wheaton, Illinois 60189. All rights reserved.

Published by Barbour Books, an imprint of Barbour Publishing, Inc., P.O. Box 719, Uhrichsville, Ohio 44683
www.barbourbooks.com

Printed in the United States of America.

Balance
FOR BUSY MOMS

For my good friends—
you know who you are—my fellow jugglers.
If you look closely, I'm sure you'll see pieces
of our conversations in this book.
Thank you for all you teach me.

INTRODUCTION
The Frustration of Juggling Our Lives

I don't know about you, but I can't seem to get everything done that I should. Oh, I can do some of the things on my "to do" list—but not all of them. There are just too many balls to juggle, and I can never keep them all spinning in the air at once.

If my professional career is going well, then you could write your name in the dust on my shelves, and the laundry pile in the basement is as tall as my youngest daughter, and my family has eaten takeout or leftovers for the last week. Or I may feel good about my involvement at church, the classes I'm teaching and the programs I'm co-ordinating—but meanwhile, my mother is hurt because I haven't had a chance to call her for the last two weeks. Or then there are the weeks when I'm feeling domestic; my house shines, and the warm smells of banana bread and homemade

9

applesauce greet anyone who comes to the door
—but my friends are starting to feel neglected
because I haven't called them, and the most inti-
mate thing I've shared with my husband recently
is the bathroom when we jostle past each other
on our way to our separate days. And then, of
course, is the biggest ball of all that I juggle: my
children. Sometimes providing them with the
care they need—keeping them clean and fed and
clothed, along with giving them love and attention—is just about the only ball I can manage to
keep up in the air.

If you're a mother, then I bet your life's not
much different from mine. All of us are jugglers.
We're housekeepers, laundresses, interior decora-
tors, counselors, confidants, nurses, cooks,
friends, chauffeurs, seamstresses, daughters, cos-
tume makers, bookkeepers, volunteers, secre-
taries, manicurists, shoppers, disciplinarians,
neighbors, referees. . . . The list goes on and on.

As modern mothers, we have a few more
balls to juggle than our mothers and grand-
mothers and great-grandmothers did: like
careers—and quality time with our children—
and the responsibility for aging parents who may
live hours away instead of around the block. But
mothers have always been jugglers, down
through the ages—and mothering has always

been exhausting. (Think about a world without supermarkets or washing machines, vacuum cleaners or refrigerators.)

One of my mother's early memories is hearing her mother ask their pastor, "How can a woman with four young children and a house to keep possibly find time for prayer?" My grandmother was always considered a "saint," so my mother remembers being astonished to hear genuine anger and frustration in her voice. And when the pastor was unable to find an answer for her, she probably turned away with tears in her eyes. I know my grandmother: She really wanted to be perfect.

This story took place sixty years ago. But as a Christian wife and mother, I can relate today to my grandmother's frustration and guilt. I think now more than ever, mothers (and particularly Christian mothers) feel called to meet our many roles with saintly perfection—and when we fail to keep all those many balls spinning smoothly and perfectly, we feel as though we have failed, not only physically but spiritually. And none of us like failure.

I believe God can use even our failures. He does not call us to be perfect; He simply calls us to be His. But I also believe we don't have to stumble through life, lunging and leaping to catch all the balls in our lives, overwhelmed as they bounce and tumble around us. Instead of being at the mercy of those balls, with the Spirit's guidance we can begin to be in control of the many parts of our busy lives.

All the books in the Juggling Our Lives series deal with time management in some form or another. The other titles, however, focus on one particular "ball" we mothers juggle—preparing meals, for instance, or our relationships with our husbands. But this book, *101 Time-Management Tips*, concentrates specifically on ways to make our entire juggling routine go more smoothly— and find time for God.

I can't offer you any magic formula to keep your life spinning effortlessly and perfectly. These are issues I struggle with as much as any-one, so I won't pretend to be the next time-management guru. But as one busy mother to another, I want to share with you the juggling principles I've found to work in my own life. These are techniques that will help us connect with God every day, strategies that will put us in control of our busy lives.

Rather than trying to put the entire book into practice all at once, start small. Even one new habit can change your life. Or try a few at a time and gradually work your way through the book. And remember—God calls each of us to carry His love to the world in our own separate ways. But He does not call any of us to perfection in our own strength. We all drop a few balls now and then—and fortunately, our God is big enough to pick them up.

So trust God's strength rather than your own—and juggle with joy!

1
Be willing to change.

As unhappy and frustrated as we may feel about our personal juggling routines, we are often reluctant to change. The way we're living our lives may not be the most productive—but at least it's familiar. We've been living this way for years, and the thought of trying something new fills us with anxiety.

And meanwhile, God tugs at us, urging us forward into a place we've never been. He created each of us to be a unique person who brings her own special gifts to His kingdom—and He wants us to pick up those gifts and use them effectively. He longs for us to stop being overwhelmed by our busy lives and instead be the people He created us to be, individuals who are free to reflect His glory.

But you can't learn to manage your time better—or anything else—unless you're willing to change.

BALANCE FOR BUSY MOMS

No one can make you change.
No one can stop you from changing.
No one really knows how you must change.
Not even you.
Not until you start.

DAVID VISCOTT

ह

It takes courage to grow up
and turn out
to be who you really are.

E. E. CUMMINGS

ह

And as the Spirit of the Lord
works within us,
we become more and more
like him and reflect
his glory even more.

2 CORINTHIANS 3:18 NLT

2
Set aside a quiet time with God to sit down and examine your life.

No matter how much we learn about time-management techniques, we'll never put the various strategies into practice until we take time to simply lay all our "balls" down for a short space. Only then will we be able step back and truly see the way we're living our lives.

Taking that first short break from your frantic routine may seem like an insurmountable obstacle. But I promise you, the world will not end if you set aside one afternoon or an evening, an hour or two when you put everything on hold while you spend some time alone with God. Use this time to look at your life from a new perspective. Consider ways you could do things differently; ask for God's insight and direction for your life. And then, in those quiet moments, be patient enough to wait for His voice speaking to your heart.

Search me, O God,
and know my heart;
test me and know my thoughts.
Point out anything in me
that offends you,
and lead me along the path
of everlasting life.

PSALM 139:23–24 NLT

3
Determine which priorities you want to be yours.

During the quiet time you spend alone with God, examine what is most important in your life. If you need some help, take a look at this list of common priorities. Number the list in order of importance from 1 to 14 to reflect honestly the way you are living your life today.

- Your marriage
- Your children
- Your reputation
- Your money
- Your job
- Your sense of control
- Your appearance
- Your health (mental, physical, spiritual)
- Your possessions
- Your pleasures
- Your friends

- Your church
- Your community
- Your relationship with God

Then renumber the list according to the way you truly long to live (not the way you think you *should* live your life; listen for God's voice deep in your heart and ignore the voices that belong to your mother, your friends, or anyone else). Insert any additional priorities you feel this list leaves out.

How can you change your life to reflect your new hierarchy of priorities? Are there any "balls" you should pick up? Are there a few God is asking you to set down?

*Set your minds on things above,
not on earthly things.*

COLOSSIANS 3:2

Whatever is at the center of our life
will be the source of our
security, guidance, wisdom, and power.

STEPHEN COVEY

What is at the center of your life?
Carefully examine where you spend
your attention, your time. . . .
This is what receives
your care and attention—
and by definition, your love.

WAYNE MULLER

ξ ξ ʃ

Juggling Tip

To help you determine your priorities on a day-to-day basis, ask yourself: "If I choose to do this activity (or not do it), how will that effect my life ten years from now?" You may find that this question will change your perspective on things. For instance, it will matter very little ten years from now whether your laundry is done today—but it may matter a great deal ten years from now if you choose today to spend time with your child—or exercise—or invest in your marriage.

4
Recognize your gifts.

One of the first steps toward using our time more effectively is to recognize our gifts—but it's a step we often fail to take. Instead, we listen to all the voices in our heads that tell us we should do this instead of that, we ought to be doing that instead of wasting our time doing this.

For instance, I'm not a particularly gifted homemaker. Although God has given me plenty of other gifts, I often use all my energy struggling to live up to that invisible housekeeping standard I keep inside my mind. No matter how I struggle, though, I never feel like much of a success, because I'm just not very talented in this particular area—and by the time I'm done with the housework, I'm sometimes too exhausted to use the gifts I do have.

Obviously, I'm going to have to do a minimum amount of homemaking, gifted or not. As much as I might sometimes like to, I can't say to my family, "Sorry, no supper tonight because I'm just not a talented cook." But I can choose to use my best hours, the hours when I'm able to truly concentrate on my work, for those things that I'm good at doing.

Of course, when I do that, I often hear this nagging little voice accusing me of wasting my time. Because the thing is, we usually enjoy the things we're good at doing; our talents give us pleasure, and so we feel guilty for having such a good time when so much other tedious work is waiting to be done.

But God gave us our talents. He doesn't want us to set them aside out of some false sense of guilt; instead, He wants us to use them for His glory. And when we do, our talents will give Him as much pleasure as they do us.

Your talent is God's gift to you.
What you do with it
is your gift back to God.

LEO BUSCAGLIA

God has given each of us the ability
to do certain things well.
So if God has given you the ability to
prophesy,
speak out when you have faith that
God is speaking through you.
If your gift is that of serving others,
serve them well.
If you are a teacher, do a good job of
teaching.
If your gift is to encourage others,
do it!
If you have money, share it generously.
If God has given you leadership ability,
take the responsibility seriously.
And if you have a gift for showing
kindness to others, do it gladly.

ROMANS 12:6–8 NLT

5
Write a personal mission statement.

Big corporations and small companies all find that a mission statement is a valuable tool for helping them structure their organizations— and almost any time-management book you pick up also recommends that individuals develop mission statements of their own. The reason is simple: A mission statement helps you be clear about how you should be using your time. It gives you direction. It's the guiding principle that makes sense of all the seemingly random elements of your life.

As a mother struggling to juggle your life, a mission statement will help you recognize your own personal vision for the future. What is your heart's desire? What do you feel God calling you to do? During your quiet time alone with God, gather your courage and ask these questions—and then be brave enough to hear the answers.

Mission statements can be short or long—it's up to you. Here are some examples:

- "My mission is to serve God by expressing my love in concrete actions to my family and to my community."
- "I will put God first and my family next. As I do this, I will never compromise my honesty, and I will practice listening to the perspectives of others. I will defend the honor of those who are not present; I will keep my sense of humor; I will take risks as God directs. I will never stop growing; each year, I will develop one new proficiency in some area of my life."
- "I aim to practice love in everything I do."
- "God has given me a vision to spread His love to those who are in need. I will share my talents, my time, my home, and my money with those who are needy, whether spiritually, physically, or emotionally."
- "My heart's desire is to experience God's peace in all areas of my life—

my home, my finances, my relationships, my career, and my community."

You may not be able to develop your mission statement in one single session alone with
God. Instead, you may need to put it on a back
burner in your mind and think about it for several days or even weeks. But I encourage you to
make an active commitment to completing this
statement.

And once you do, put your mission in writing. Place it somewhere you will see it often—on
the wall over your washing machine, beside your
computer, on the visor of your car, or in your
daily planner. Knowing your mission in life will
help you choose more wisely which things you
should be juggling. It will help you to manage
your time more effectively.

Vision is of God.
A vision comes in advance
of any task well done.

KATHERINE LOGAN

6
Set goals that will help make your vision real.

Once you have completed your mission statement, the next step is to determine the goals that will bring your vision out of your heart and into the world. Goals are the concrete actions we take to put flesh on our vision, to make it live and breathe in our families and communities.

Here are some examples of goals:

- I will set aside time each week to spend with each of my children.
- I will take a class that will help me grow in my profession.
- I will join a prayer group.
- I will set aside regular times each day to spend alone with God.
- I will participate in an exercise class, get regular sleep, and establish healthier eating patterns so that I

will no longer be so tired.

- I will hire someone to do some of my cleaning and use my extra time to develop a talent God has given me.
- I will organize a baby-sitting cooperative with other young mothers so we can have more free time for ourselves.
- I will spend one evening a week with my husband.
- I will delegate some of my work to others so I can have more energy for my God-given gifts.

Your goals will be uniquely your own. Again, as with your mission statement, write your goals down somewhere you can refer to them often. Be accountable to them. Allow them to direct your individual juggling routine.

Forgetting what is behind and
straining toward what is ahead,
I press on toward the goal to win the prize
for which God has
called me heavenward in Christ Jesus.

THE APOSTLE PAUL (PHILIPPIANS 3:13–14)

7
Evaluate the set of "balls" you're currently juggling in light of your priorities, goals, and personal mission statement.

During your time alone with God, write down all the roles and responsibilities you are currently juggling—those things that use up your time on any given day.

Now look at each item in light of your priorities, goals, and mission. Does each "ball" fit into the structure you've been developing for your life? Or is much of your time taken up with things that have little real importance to you?

If you find a "ball" that has nothing to do with your priorities, your goals, or your mission, seriously consider: Can you put this "ball" down? What would Jesus want you to do?

O Lord, may I be directed
what to do and what to leave undone.

ELIZABETH FRY

〜〜

*The main thing is to keep
the main thing the main thing.*

STEPHEN COVEY

〜〜

Things which matter most
must never be put at the mercy of
things which matter least.

GOETHE

8
Make yearly, monthly, weekly, and daily plans.

You may find that your goals and your plans are very similar—but plans tend to be more concrete and specific. A goal might be: "Spend regular time alone with God." The plan tells when and where you will make that happen: "I will go to my room on Sunday evening between seven and nine o'clock to be alone with God."

Before I was a mother and author, I used to be a special education teacher—and as a teacher, I wouldn't have dreamed of heading into a school week without my weekly plan book all filled out. Real life (and a classroom of children) meant that my plans often had to be modified—but at least they were there, a structure to work from and build on, a guide to keep me pointed in the right direction when otherwise I'd have been too busy to keep track of where I was going.

My plan book provided a pattern for my

workday juggling. I still dropped balls, of course; even the most skillful juggler does sometimes. But when I did, I could simply pick up the ball and keep going—or I could choose to let it roll off into the corner temporarily. Either way, the pattern was there, and I could go on with my day smoothly.

As a mother, I often just "wing it." I muddle through my life, seeing each day as a jumbled mass of kids and housework and professional responsibilities. But when I do that, I lack a pattern to keep me on track when the balls start slipping out of my hands. Lunging and stretching for those balls, trying desperately to keep up with everything, my relationship with God slips farther and farther into the background. Christ's presence is no longer living and real for me—and I've forgotten what my mission is all about.

We all have days when we can't keep up with our juggling routines. But if we have our plans already well mapped ahead of time, we can get back on track far more easily and quickly.

Any enterprise is built by wise planning,
becomes strong through common sense,
and profits wonderfully by
keeping abreast of the facts.

PROVERBS 24:3–4 TLB

*Planning is bringing the future
into the present
so that you can do something
about it now.*

ALAN LAKEIN

9
Recognize the false assumptions that are ruling your life, and make a conscious effort to let them go.

- The more you accomplish, the more worthy a person you are.

- I'm the only one who can do it right.

- I can do it all—take care of my family, be at the top of my career, keep my home spotless, be a good friend, be active in my church, be there for my parents. . .

- The busier you are, the more people respect you.

- I'm a failure if my house is a mess.

- I have to do everything perfectly or it doesn't count.

We all have false assumptions like these floating around in our heads. They're like the voices of imaginary gods we try desperately to placate. We're probably not even conscious of what we're doing, but that doesn't make those imaginary gods any less powerful. In fact, the more unconscious we are, the tighter the gods will squeeze our lives.

But God doesn't want us to listen to any god's voice but His. So the first step toward denying those imaginary gods their power is to make a list of the lies they've been telling you, the ones you've been listening to so slavishly. This isn't easy; you may need help from a friend, and then you'll need time and quiet to truly examine your heart. Ask the Spirit for His insight.

When you stop ordering your life in obedience to your personal set of false assumptions, you'll find you have more time for your true priorities.

Then you will know the truth,
and the truth will set you free.

JESUS OF NAZARETH (JOHN 8:32)

10
Make God your focus
no matter what you're doing.

Sometimes we simply can't seem to make time in our lives for God. We try hard to pick up this shining "ball" that gleams with such heavenly light—and yet it seems so heavy. All too easily, we let it roll into the corners of our lives where it sits quietly gathering dust. After all, the other "balls" clamor for our attention with such insistence. God doesn't give us deadlines; He doesn't tug on our sleeves or ring our doorbells or send us late notices in the mail; and His voice is so small and still that the loud voices of others drown Him out.

But when we think like this, we're operating with another false assumption. God isn't one more ball we somehow have to squeeze into our already crowded routines. Instead, He is the force that holds all the other pieces of our busy lives together. On the busiest, most chaotic days, His presence is the still point at the center of it all.

When I first started writing and speaking to mothers about juggling, I saw it as a metaphor for the frustration of our lives. But as I read about the actual physical practice of juggling, I realized that it's also a metaphor of hope. Steve Cohen, a professional juggler, says, "Juggling takes many elements and creates a cohesive, unified, manageable system. . .forged of thoughtful choices pieced together to establish a new unity." In other words, a juggler's focus is not on the individual pieces she is juggling; it's on something bigger, something outside the twirling objects above her head.

As I apply that thought to my own life, I realize that God is the cohesive force that makes a "new unity" out of all the other pieces of my life. He is not merely one more piece in the pattern; instead, He is the one to whom I offer my entire whirling, bouncing, chaotic life. And as I offer it up to Him, He transforms it into a "unified, manageable system."

What a relief! Because when I look at my life from this new perspective, things become far simpler. On any given day—whether I have one thing on my to-do list or twenty—in reality I have only one responsibility: To keep my eyes fixed on Jesus.

In everything you do, put God first,
and he will direct you and
crown your efforts with success.

PROVERBS 3:6 TLB

}{

Let us fix our eyes on Jesus.

HEBREWS 12:2

}{

The time of business does not with me
differ from the time of prayer;
and in the noise and clatter of my kitchen,
while several persons are at the same time
calling for different things, I possess God
in as great tranquility as if I were on my knees.

BROTHER LAWRENCE

11
Know you are not alone in your struggles with time.

If I'd had any lingering illusions that I might, after all, be destined to become the next time-management guru, they would have been rudely shattered yesterday. I was busily writing about ways we can juggle our lives more smoothly, when my phone rang. The person on the line let me know I had definitely dropped a "ball." My son had participated in a special program after school—and I had failed to pick him up. What made my embarrassment and dismay all the greater was the fact that this was the third time I had forgotten to pick him up from this particular activity.

My face red, I rushed into school, overflowing with apologies to both my son and the teachers involved. I expected my son to be worried and upset—but instead, I found him happily playing in a corner of the room with his best friend.

Seems the friend's mother had forgotten him, too. I suppose it wasn't very mature of me to be delighted by someone else's failure—but I was.

Sometimes I feel as though no one else in the whole world is as disorganized as I am. Everyone else's life seems to go so easily and smoothly, while I dash around like a chicken with my head cut off. I suspect I must have some deep congenital flaw that keeps me from handling my time with consistent ease and grace.

I long to be like my favorite saints, women like Susanna Wesley, Teresa of Avila, Julian of Norwich, and Amy Carmichael. I imagine these women living quiet lives of glowing calm, sailing through their days on a deep sea of serenity. If only I could be like them. . . .

But the truth is this: Even the great saints struggled to manage their time. They all had conflicting demands on their lives; they all struggled to be true to their personal vision in the midst of life's ordinary humdrum responsibilities. In fact, I'll bet even the genuine time-management gurus—the people who make their living telling the rest of us how to manage our time more efficiently—still struggle occasionally to practice what they preach.

Of course there are skills we can learn, habits we can form, and techniques we can cultivate that will help our juggling routines go far more easily. But ultimately, we're still juggling. And juggling by its very definition isn't a particular pattern of action you can learn once and then be done with it. Instead, juggling is an activity that's ongoing, always developing. The juggler never gets to smugly say, "There, I got that mastered"; instead, juggling requires constant effort and focus. If even the most proficient juggler looks away from her routine for just a moment, her balls will come tumbling down.

We all experience struggles with time management. It's part of the human condition.

I am always stealing the time [for spiritual and intellectual pursuits] and that with great difficulty, for it hinders me from spinning and I. . .have numerous other things to do.

TERESA OF AVILA

*Many people, greatly desiring
the life of communion with God,
find no opportunity for attention
to Him in an existence which often
lacks privacy and is conditioned
by ceaseless household duties,
exacting professional responsibilities,
or long hours of work.
The great spiritual teachers,
who are not nearly so aloof
from normal life as those who
do not read them suppose,
have often dealt with this situation. . . .*

EVELYN UNDERHILL

12
Remember: Juggling our lives is not a competitive sport.

My neighbor's house is always spotless. I have never gone to her door unexpectedly and found her floors anything but gleaming and clutter-free. Then there's my sister; she's a wonderful mother, a professional who's respected in her field, a church leader, the school board president, and a good friend to a large circle of women (including her little sister). And my mother-in-law is even worse. She's one of those women who cook and clean as easily as they breathe, and at seventy, her energy level far exceeds mine. When I consider people like these, I never fail to reach a depressing conclusion: I just don't measure up.

But then this summer at a writers' conference, I was startled when a woman came up to me and said, "I want you to know I hate you. When I look at all the books you've written and then hear you talk about your three young children, I get so depressed. How do you find time to be both a mother and an author? You must be the most organized person alive."

Well, I thought, *you haven't seen my laundry room. . . .*

The truth is, it's easy to be impressed by the juggling routines of those around us. We see the set of "balls" they're keeping up in the air so efficiently—and we don't know that they've got another set bouncing on the floor in their dark corners.

To help me grasp this concept, I imagine three women juggling side by side in a row. The woman on one end is tossing three rubber balls up and down, the next one is juggling a dozen plates, and the last one is keeping two raw eggs up in the air. Now suppose the one in the middle, the one with the dozen plates, spends all her time eying the other two women. *Look at that,* she thinks to herself as she watches the woman with the three rubber balls, *look how smoothly she juggles. She never drops a ball. I wish I could be like her. . .* And then she turns to the other direction and thinks, *Look at her—she's juggling eggs. They're so fragile—and yet she hasn't dropped one. If only I could juggle so well. . .* And meanwhile, of course, the woman's thoughts are interrupted again and again by the sound of something crashing to the floor. She simply can't keep all those plates up in the air. Especially not when her focus is on the juggling routines of others rather than her own.

The point is this: It really doesn't matter how your juggling routine compares to anyone else's. One person may seem to live life more smoothly simply because the things she's juggling don't require as much effort. Or she may have learned her limitations; she knows that the rigorous demands of her life require her to focus on only one or two things at a time. We each juggle a unique set of roles and responsibilities, and God loves us all equally, no matter how many times our lives seem to come crashing down around us. We are not competing with each other.

And worrying about how we compare with others will only make us lose our focus on our own juggling routines.

Let me remember that
each life must follow its own course,
and that what happens to other people
has absolutely nothing to do with
what happens to me.

MARJORIE HOLMES

13
*View time management as
a positive experience, something that
will give you more freedom.*

Sometimes, I look at time management as one more item on a to-do list that's already endless. There it is: *Organize my time,* right after *Read to the kids* and before *Clean the house.* I feel exhausted just thinking about this one more duty I should be accomplishing.

But I'm learning to ignore the word should when I hear it echoing in my heart. I've come to realize that the Holy Spirit doesn't "should" us. When I hear a voice whispering, *You should do this. . . You ought to do that. . . ,* it's not God; in fact, it's probably the Enemy of my soul, the Accuser who wants to convince us all that we're worthless and guilty.

If you look at time management as something you should do, then chances are you think, *If only I managed my time better, I'd get so much more accomplished.* Well, yes, that's one benefit of time management. But this book is not intended to be a tool that will help you become a long-suffering martyr who juggles umpteen balls, plates, swords, and flaming torches. Instead, my goal is to remind us all (myself included) to juggle only what God wants, to create a juggling routine that will give Him (and us) the greatest joy.

When the Spirit whispers in our hearts, His words bring joy and life. Learning to manage our time more efficiently is one way we become free to enjoy the many blessings He's given to us all.

*Effective time management means
having time left over to do
the things you want to do.
It gives you time to spend
with family and friends,
to be creative and enjoy life.*

LEE SILBER

14
Put your excuses in God's hands.

I just don't have time to organize my time right now, because. . .

> I'm not feeling well.
> I'm in the midst of a family crisis.
> I have too many professional demands.
> It would take too much time.

We all have a set of excuses that explains why we don't start practicing better time-management techniques. For most of us, what it comes down to is this: Like the Duchess in *Alice in Wonderland,* we're all running as fast as we can just to stay in one place. Our lives are so busy that we can't stop long enough to evaluate our priorities and formulate a mission statement; we're so frantic, so desperate to accomplish all that's expected of us, that setting aside even an hour to look at our lives in the light of God's presence seems like an unrealistic waste of time. Like drowning people in a raging sea, we're treading water so furiously, just barely managing to keep our heads above the water, that we can't bring ourselves to stop long enough to grab the life preserver someone has thrown to us.

But you don't have to live like this. God wants to offer you safety from those tossing waves. Take your excuses and put them one by one in God's hands. This may take an act of blind faith and sheer determination—but you can trust Him. He won't let you drown.

Come to me, all you who are weary and burdened, and I will give you rest.

JESUS OF NAZARETH (MATTHEW 11:28)

❧

Dump the excuses.
They just get in the way of
recognizing the important things,
setting realistic priorities,
and creating the life you want to be living.

LEE SILBER

15
Expect that at first managing your time more productively will not come easily. Learning any new skill takes time and discipline.

We live in a culture that expects things easily and quickly. Fast-food restaurants, timesaving technology, and instant everything all promise that we can have what we want right now. We try a new way of living—and then quickly give up the first time we fail. After all, we don't like failure; it's embarrassing and humiliating, and we'd rather not try again if we're just going to mess things up. We might not expect to sit down at the piano and become a concert pianist overnight— but we do expect that we can become overnight maestros of time management. We have forgotten that most of the truly valuable things in life take time and disciplined effort.

Brother Lawrence, the seventeenth-century author of *The Practice of the Presence of God,* was a juggler extraordinaire. We might imagine that Brother Lawrence found it easy to keep his focus constantly on God; after all, he lived in a monastery in a far simpler time than ours. But in reality, Brother Lawrence faced his own set of challenges. He was the monastery cook, responsible for feeding a large "family" in a time when cooking involved hard physical labor. He had every intention of living in God's presence moment by moment—but too often, the noise and demands of his job intruded on his thoughts of Jesus. In fact, he wrote that it took him ten years of dedicated practice before he learned to consistently live in God's presence. Even then, he still lost his focus from time to time. But Brother Lawrence did not let that bother him. He wrote:

> I worshipped Him as often as I could, keeping my mind focused on His holy presence and calling my attention back whenever I found myself being distracted. This exercise was not easy, and yet I continued in it, in spite of how hard it was, without worrying or feeling guilty every time my thoughts wandered. I worked at this all day long, not only during prayer times, for at all times, every hour, every minute, even in the midst of my busiest

*times, I drove out of my mind anything
that might distract me from thoughts
from God.*

*. . .Practicing this over and over, it
becomes a habit, and the presence of God
becomes the natural condition for us.*

When I consider that Brother Lawrence needed ten years to reach the degree of saintliness I read between the lines of his writing, I'm tempted to throw up my hands in frustration and discouragement. After all, I make no claims to being a saint.

But God doesn't expect us to be transformed into Brother Lawrence's clones. All He wants is for us to be diligent and disciplined with the gifts He's given us. And meanwhile, *He* will transform us—into the image of His Son.

*I never could have done
what I have done
without the habit of
punctuality, order, and diligence.*

CHARLES DICKENS

*Without discipline,
there's no life at all.*

KATHERINE HEPBURN

〉〉〉

Never be lacking in zeal,
but keep your spiritual fervor,
serving the Lord.

ROMANS 12:11

16
Don't be afraid to fail.

If a toddler refused to learn to walk because she might fall, she would spend the rest of her life on her hands and knees. She'd look pretty silly creeping onto the school bus when she went to kindergarten—and even more foolish when she crawled across the stage to accept her diploma at her high school graduation.

Very few of us can take off running with a brand-new skill. Most of us take a single step—and then plop down on our behinds. But if we struggle to our feet, we'll find the next time we're able to go a few steps farther before we're once more down on the floor. Each failure teaches us something about ourselves and the skill we're learning. And if we persist, one day we'll find ourselves running, skipping, maybe even leaping and jumping as we become still more proficient.

The only true failure is simply to sit on the floor and give up.

*There is the greatest
practical benefit in making a
few failures early in life.*

THOMAS HENRY HUXLEY

I was never afraid of failure,
for I would sooner fail than
not be among the greatest.

JOHN KEATS

17
Accept that you will never totally conquer time.

I like to be good at what I do. So I don't like to try a new skill unless I think I will be able to master it completely.

But no matter how skillful a person becomes at managing her time, no matter how many new timesaving habits she cultivates, no matter how disciplined she is as she practices her juggling routine, occasionally time will continue to elude her. It will slip through her fingers when she's not looking; it will run away from her despite her best efforts to control it; and its limitations will take her by surprise when she least expects them.

So I have to accept that ultimately I can never totally manage time. Given that, I can continue to be frustrated by my weakness—or I can choose simply to let go of my need for control. When I do, then I am free to relax in God's hands. Safe and secure, I can be amazed and delighted by time's surprises.

After all, God is the one who created time in the first place—and He is the one whose power extends far beyond time's boundaries.

Life is not orderly (or perfect).
It is rich and fascinating
and exciting,
and meant to be lived to its fullest.

LEE SILBER

He did not say,
"You shall not be tempest-tossed,
you shall not be work-weary,
you shall not be discomforted."
But he said, "You shall not be overcome."

JULIAN OF NORWICH

18
*Set aside time
(on a weekly, monthly, or,
at the very least, yearly basis)
to reevaluate your juggling routine.
Include God in the process.*

These juggling acts of ours are not something we can get right once and for all. Life is always throwing new "balls" into the set we're already juggling. No matter how carefully we may have formulated our goals, priorities, and mission statements, before we know it, we will find ourselves overwhelmed once more.

When that happens, we'll probably feel like throwing up our hands in frustration. *Well, that certainly didn't work,* we'll say to ourselves.

Really, though, we simply need to set aside another time with God to take a new look at our lives. We may need to evaluate our priorities all over again; we may even find we want to expand or modify our mission statements. When we do, we'll probably find we need to sort again the "balls" we're juggling. If new elements have been added to our lives, we'll need to decide whether we should keep them—or set them down. If we feel God has called us to these new "balls," then we may need to see how we can adjust our routine to realistically allow for the added items.

We can wait to do all this until we're so desperate we can't function anymore—but it makes more sense to simply schedule these recurring "planning sessions" ahead of time, on a weekly, monthly, or—at a minimum—yearly basis. Juggling isn't something we can do on autopilot.

I will instruct you and teach you
in the way you should go;
I will counsel you and watch over you.

PSALM 32:8

19
Using a calendar or daily planner, make a weekly agenda.

Be realistic when you do this; remember, there are only 168 hours in any week (and you should be asleep for about 56 of those hours). Be sure that each day's agenda supports your personal mission statement. If it doesn't, evaluate whether a particular activity is truly necessary.

A friend of mine suggested I use this image to help me structure my time: If I were filling a jar with different sized stones and I put the smallest ones in the jar first, I might find I had no room at the end for the large ones. But if I did it the other way around and put the largest ones in first, then I could fill in the empty spaces with the smaller stones.

A week is the container into which we must put an assortment of different tasks. Each activity has a different "size," and arranging them in our days is a simple process of putting in the most important tasks first, and then fitting as many small ones as we can around those more important activities. As we evaluate which tasks lie ahead, we need to calculate the size of each job and whether we can realistically fit it into the space we have available.

Sometimes, though, we fail to understand the size of our container. We act as though a week were a bottomless jar. With enough determination, we surmise, we should be able to fit it all in. And so we press and cram and squeeze—and then wonder why we find our nights becoming shorter and shorter. *There just aren't enough days in the week,* we complain to ourselves.

Actually, though, the week has all the days it needs. We simply need to accept that time is a finite thing—and a planner will help us see more clearly the week's boundaries.

*Don't act thoughtlessly,
but try to understand what
the Lord wants you to do.*

EPHESIANS 5:17 NLT

*A schedule defends from
chaos and whim.
It is a net for catching days.*

ANNIE DILLARD

≀≀≀

Four types of planners:

- appointment books
- wall or desk calendars
- computer programs
- handheld electronic planners

20
Keep a family calendar and integrate it with your personal planner.

The mind is an amazing thing. It is perfectly capable of keeping two parallel calendars and never integrating the two. That's why I can look at my family calendar and see that tomorrow I plan to attend my second-grader's family field day, and all the while also be planning to spend the day working with a colleague on a project. After all, I have one commitment written neatly in my work planner, while the other one is right there on my family calendar. And then suddenly I find myself saying with a sinking feeling, "Oh, you meant *that* tomorrow!"

Our family obligations are not neatly segregated in their own separate time zone. That's why we need to make sure our weekly planners accurately portray all the responsibilities we need to remember.

BALANCE FOR BUSY MOMS

Things to include in your family calendar:

- School events
- Parent-teacher meetings
- Anything special your child needs to bring to school on a particular day
- Birthday parties (include time and place)
- Sports events (both games and practices)
- After-school activities
- Music lessons
- Doctors' and dentists' appointments
- Vacations

21
Coordinate a week's worth of menus with your weekly agenda. Base your weekly shopping list on these menus

I find that if I wait until the end of my work-day to think about supper, my mind—and usually my cupboard—is completely empty. But if I make a weekly plan, the hard part—thinking what to have—is already done. And if my weekly grocery trip was based on this plan, then I'll find the ingredients already waiting in my cupboard.

〈〉〈

Juggling Tip:

If you know you have a particularly busy week ahead, this might be a good weekend to cook on the weekend and freeze some ready-made casseroles.

22

Make a daily to-do list and keep it somewhere you can refer to it often throughout the day— on your computer, on your calendar, in your daily planner.

Divide your list into number-one priorities (things that have to be done today), number-two priorities (things that have to be done sooner or later this week), and number-three priorities (things that it would be nice to accomplish, but the world won't end if you don't).

Include appointments for both yourself and your family members in this list. Otherwise, you may forget something important. Also, this will help you see how much time you really have in your day. If your daughter has a doctor's appointment in the morning, you have a work conference in the afternoon, and your son's Little League game is in the evening, realistically, the rest of your to-do list should be pretty short.

*If you don't have a
single reliable to-do list or planner,
chances are you won't get
to many of your important tasks
simply because you can't remember
that you have to do them!*

JULIE MORGENSTERN

23
As much as possible,
include the activities you enjoy most
in each day's top priorities.

Remember—our talents were given to us by God for us to enjoy and use. They enable us to live out our mission statements. So it only makes sense that these activities, the ones we truly love to do (rather than scrubbing the toilet, for instance), should be our top priorities.

That doesn't mean we should never clean our toilets. (In fact, if things get really bad, we may find a clean toilet becomes a definite priority!) But on most days, we can probably look at household chores like cleaning the toilet as the gravel we allow to filter around the gaps left by our lives' larger tasks.

If your deepest heart is calling you to a particular activity, don't try to fit it in after you've done all the many tedious tasks that can consume your life. Instead, reserve the hours when you have the most energy for this heart-calling. Make it a number-one priority.

You need to focus what energy you have on things you are passionate about. And you need some level of time management and organization to keep you from getting distracted and wasting yourself on the small stuff.

LEE SILBER

24
Make a weekly appointment with God.

Like Brother Lawrence, we too can learn to practice the continual presence of God. Our entire lives—including our professions, our relationships, and even our housework—can become love offerings to Jesus.

But that doesn't mean we don't need to write God's name on a specific day in our weekly agendas. Although He is with us constantly, our human brains and hearts need to set aside time when we can focus on Him without distraction, time when we can gather support and encouragement from others, time when we can learn more about our faith and ourselves in relation to God.

Most of us find that Sunday morning church services are the place and time where these needs are met. No matter how busy we are, most weeks we need to keep this appointment with God.

Let us not give up
meeting together,
as some are
in the habit of doing,
but let us encourage
one another. . . .

HEBREWS 10:25

25
Set aside a piece of time in each day for God.

We humans are so easily distracted. No matter how clear we may think we are about our priorities and mission, we often set out in the morning with one plan for juggling, only to find by nightfall that we've lost track of all our good intentions.

That's why we need to take at least some small moments each day when we consciously set aside all the things we juggle and come into God's presence. Each of us will find that a different time may work best. For some it may be the half hour before the rest of the household wakes up; others will use their lunch hours as their special time with God; and still others may find that late at night before they go to bed is the only time when they feel calm enough to hear God's voice. Whenever and wherever, these moments help us maintain our focus throughout the day. We leave these times better able to pick up our routines and juggle smoothly.

Some days may be so hectic that we find ourselves missing these quiet moments altogether. When that happens, we can still snatch a few moments for prayer. . .while we shower, while we drive, or while we do some mindless chore.

God is always with us, regardless of what we are doing. It is our own hearts that need reminding.

Because I am a woman
involved in practical cares,
I cannot give the first half of
the day to [spiritual matters],
but must [pray] when I can,
early in the morning,
on the fly during the day.
Not in privacy. . . but here, there,
and everywhere—
at the kitchen table. . .on my way
to and from appointments
and even while making supper or
putting [my daughter] to bed.

DOROTHY DAY

26
Schedule at least a little time in each day that's just for you.

In the midst of writing this book, ironically I found myself most in need of this particular time-management technique. A friend interrupted my work with this E-mail message: "Let me ask you—what are you doing that doesn't mean work. . .something that simply gives you joy? Find the answer and do a little of it each day. We are no good when we are in need of refreshment or nourishment, at least that is what I find with my garden. The plants need nourishment and water or they droop and lose their beauty. Are we so different? Please be kind to yourself. . . people love you and need you. You are efficient and talented. . .but you can do the work in half the time if you are refreshed!"

She was right of course. But this is a difficult strategy for most women to practice. We're so conditioned to give and give and give that we feel guilty taking time for something frivolous, something we simply enjoy doing. *Maybe someday*, we think to ourselves, *when I have time. . .* But face it, we'll never have time if we don't make time. We need to write our own names in our daily planner (in ink, not pencil), or we'll never find the time.

Most days, these personal moments may be as brief and simple as a hot bath at the end of the day—or a walk during lunch—or a cup of coffee at our favorite little café on our way to work. Occasionally, though, our personal pleasures may be more time-consuming—a book we've been wanting to read, a seminar we've been longing to attend, a night out with an old friend. These events seem so trivial that we feel foolish insisting we need these small treats.

But the fact is, we do need them. We cannot continue to give to those we love, if we never give to ourselves. And oddly enough, we may be surprised to find that our best ideas, our most productive strategies, and the deepest stirrings of God's grace come to us in the midst of these moments of self-indulgence.

*A little of what you fancy
does you good.*

Marie Lloyd

27
Surrender all the "balls" you juggle to God.

I'm very good at maintaining two conflicting perspectives at one and the same time. On the one hand, I truly want God to be the central focus of my juggling routine—and on the other hand, I want to keep my own control of a particular aspect of my life. *Don't ask me for that ball, God,* my heart whispers. *That one's all mine.*

That's why in my quiet moments alone with God, I need to make a conscious effort to give Him each and every thing I juggle. Sometimes I visualize myself laying each "ball" in His loving and capable hands. His fingers are big enough to hold them all.

When I pick my life up and begin to juggle again, I find that the "balls" have all been transformed. Even the heaviest ones seem lighter somehow. The ones that seemed so dull now shine. And I find that my favorite ones, the ones that were so difficult for me to surrender, have a new beauty that fills my heart with joy.

The tasks themselves haven't actually changed, of course—but my motivation has. Now each "ball" belongs to God.

*Our sanctification does not depend on
our changing our work,
but in doing that for God's sake
which we commonly do for our own.*

BROTHER LAWRENCE

Whatever you do,
do it all for the glory of God.

1 CORINTHIANS 10:31

೨೪

What is asked of us is not necessarily
a great deal of time devoted to
what we regard as spiritual things,
but the constant offering of our wills to God,
so that the practical duties which fill most
of our days can become part of His order
and be given spiritual worth.

EVELYN UNDERHILL

There has been a tendency
to think of service to God as necessarily
entailing physical hardship
and sacrifice.
Although this is not really a scriptural idea,
it has gained wide acceptance.
It is easy to recall the saints who climbed the
steep ascent of heaven through peril, toil,
and pain, but the Bible also makes mention
of Dorcas whose service to God
was the making of coats.

ELISABETH ELLIOT

28

Live in the moment. (In other words, don't anticipate future "balls" or try to keep your grasp on past "balls.")

As women who juggle our lives, we need to let go of both the past and the future; we need to live right now, in the present moment God has given us. A juggler who focuses on upcoming "balls," wastes her time and energy anticipating what lies ahead, while a juggler who refuses to release her hold on past "balls" will inevitably find the elements of her life beginning to pile up around her—and eventually they'll begin bouncing on the floor, while she scrambles to pick them up.

Don't worry about the job coming up next week or tomorrow—or later today. Don't fret about what you may have done wrong on the work you just completed. Instead, release them both into God's hands. Focus on the moment He's given you this instant. Don't let the past and future rob you of the time God's given you now.

BALANCE FOR BUSY MOMS

Love the moment,
and the energy of that moment
will spread. . . .

CORITA KENT

≀≀≀

*It is only possible to live
happily ever after
on a moment-by-moment basis.*

MARGARET BONNANO

≀≀≀

Let me tell thee,
time is a very precious gift of God;
so precious that He only gives it to us
moment by moment.
He would not have thee waste it.

AMELIA BARR

29
Choose to stay on task.

Most mornings I start out with a plan for a productive day—but then something happens along the way. The phone rings, and before I know it, I find I've spent an hour talking with a friend. Then the mail comes, and I get immersed with responding to a query from the insurance company. Next, I hear the little chime that tells me, "You've got mail"—and I spend the next hour dealing with a question someone needs me to answer on a particular project. I look at the clock and realize I only have another hour before my kids come home from school. With a sense of desperation, I turn back to my computer. That's when the doorbell rings. . . .

But I need not be at the mercy of circumstances; I need not allow them to dictate my days. Some things truly can't wait, but many interruptions don't need to be dealt with immediately. Instead, I can choose to handle whatever it is later, while I maintain my focus on the task at hand.

*All of us must quickly carry out
the tasks assigned us by
the one who sent me.*

JESUS OF NAZARETH (JOHN 9:4 NLT)

Juggling Tip:

Set aside a time each day when it will be convenient for you to answer phone messages and E-mail. If possible, block out chunks of your day for tasks that require more long-term concentration; do not answer the phone or check your E-mail during these times.

30
Be flexible enough to sometimes set your agenda aside.

This seems to be a contradiction to time-management tip number 29—"Choose to stay on task." But some interruptions—like a sick child, a friend who's hurting, or a lunch invitation from a husband—need to be accepted with grace. We do not know what we may miss if we are so locked in by our carefully planned schedules that we fail to open our hearts to those who need us—or to pleasures that are offered us.

After all, an agenda is just a tool designed to help us manage our time more effectively—and a tool is meant to serve its owner, not vice versa. Don't be a slave to your daily planner. God may have something else planned for you today.

Keep your agenda on your back burner.
In other words,
know what it is you would
ideally like to accomplish
but let go of your attachment
to getting it done.
Then, when possible,
gently seize the opportunities
you have to work toward those goals.

RICHARD CARLSON

31
If you feel called to a new activity, make space for it in your life.

If you're already juggling seventeen million balls, odds are you're not going to be able to pick up one more thing, no matter how beautiful or worthwhile that particular ball may be. You may be a skilled and efficient juggler, but like anyone else, you have limitations. No one can juggle seventeen million and one balls.

So if you feel your heart tugging you toward something new—and if you sense God's voice in your longing—you will need to set some "balls" down before you'll be able to pick up that new activity.

You may find that God will ask you to come back to those set-aside balls later in your life; or He may be saying to you, *You're done with that. It's time to go on to something new.* Either way, ask Him to show you which activities in your busy schedule need to be set aside—and then release them into His hands. His grasp is far bigger than ours, and we can trust Him to take care of whatever we give Him.

When we do, we are free to pick up that new shiny ball and toss it high.

If you want something to happen,
you have to make space for it.

DAVID CAMPBELL

You will never *find* time for anything.
If you want time, you must take it.

CHARLES BURTON

32
Make time for your "inner child."

The concept of the "inner child" is a popular one among self-help authors today. According to this way of thinking, all of us have a child who still lives inside us, a child who is sometimes wounded and frustrated—and sometimes delighted and full of wonder. We grown-up mothers have often learned to ignore the voices of those little girls who live in our hearts; we have too many other voices clamoring for our attention to feel justified listening to that small insistent voice inside us. In fact, we often feel guilty when we give in and listen to the demands of those interior little girls.

But God loves those little girls as much as He loves all the other children in our families. He looks at each child that's been hidden away in a grown-up heart, and He longs to gather her close. *Come out, Beloved,* He urges. *Come to Me. Come play.*

Like many mothers, I often feel ashamed when the little girl inside me cries or demands her own way. As a mother who juggles my life, I also find myself juggling attitudes about that life. On the one hand, I genuinely want to give of myself to those around me. My faith and my own self-expectations ask that I sacrifice my selfish desires for the needs of my family. But on the other hand, I was also born into a culture that insists on individual rights. The demands placed on me as a mother sometimes seem more like slavery than servanthood. I resent being the family picker-upper, rescuer, cook, and bottle-washer. As I juggle these conflicting points of view, I swing back and forth between guilt and resentment.

But I have found that if I think of my own inner child as one more member of our family, I no longer have to keep either of these "balls" aloft. As loving mothers, we would not insist that one member of the family do all the work. Treating each child fairly is a constant challenge, but we would never knowingly expect one family member to always be at the mercy of all the others. I suspect God would like us to treat our own inner children with the same fairness. As we listen to His voice, He will help us find the balance between our own needs and the needs of others. Both will be nurtured and affirmed by His loving hand.

As I practice taking care of that little girl inside my heart, listening to her needs, I find that I am able to manage my time more efficiently. When the child inside me sees the bright sunshine outside the window and cries out for a walk, I often discover I work more creatively after I grant her request. When she's tired and cranky, I get more done if I make sure she gets the rest she needs. And when she's angry because things just aren't fair, she usually has a valid point. That's when I need to reevaluate the situation—because when we mothers become the family doormats, it's really not good for anyone!

It's preserving and enhancing the greatest asset you have—you. It's renewing the four dimensions of your nature— physical, spiritual, mental, and social/emotional.

STEPHEN COVEY

33
Try to remember that Eternity is your home.

We are creatures born into Time the way a fish is born into water. Our brains are so immersed in Time that we find it difficult to even think about a world where it does not exist. When we try to talk about Eternity, we imagine never-ending Time, rather than nonexistent Time. We cannot divorce ourselves from Time any more than a fish could decide to jump out of the water and live on land.

But just because a fish can't visualize the world of air, doesn't mean the air isn't real. In the same way, Eternity is real—and unlike a fish who will die outside of water, we human beings were created to ultimately make our home in Eternity.

Deadlines and appointments, schedules and time frames, due dates and calendars, hours and days and weeks and years. . . . They all seem so real to us, so important. We live our lives within their framework. But one day we will leave them all behind. They will drop away and be forgotten forever.

There is no rush in Eternity, no hurry-up pressure. On your busiest, most frantic days, remind yourself that no matter how time rushes you along, your soul is designed for Eternity. Even now, even here, in the midst of your most desperate juggling routine, Eternity is your home.

The action of those whose
lives are given to the Spirit
has in it something of
the leisure of Eternity;
and because of this,
they achieve far more than
those whose lives are enslaved by
the rush and hurry,
the unceasing tick-tick of the world.

EVELYN UNDERHILL

34
Practice a light touch as you juggle.
Take time to laugh.

Juggling is a game. The word comes from the Latin word for "jest" or "joke," and juggling was meant to be something we do with laughter and grace. We tend to take ourselves so seriously, though, as though the entire world depended on our juggling perfectly. With an attitude like this, no wonder we see each dropped ball as a major crisis.

That sort of thinking just makes us juggle that much less smoothly, however. Stressed and pressured, we will lose our rhythm, and the balls will begin to scatter on the floor around us. But in the light of Eternity, does it really matter if our living room is not vacuumed, or we missed an appointment, or our children have no matching socks because we haven't done the laundry?

As we learn to live more consistently in God's presence, then we will begin to absorb His perspectives on life. His joy will be ours. And the next time we drop a ball, we may even find ourselves laughing.

Find someone who can juggle
five of anything,
and watch the quickness,
agile dexterity,
and focused strength it takes
to be a silly juggler.

STEVE COHEN

*Angels fly because
they take themselves lightly.*

AUTHOR UNKNOWN

}}{

Being playful is a joyful quality. . . .
It reminds you to not take yourself,
or the other members of your family,
too seriously.
. . .It allows you to keep your heart
open to those around you
and to bounce back from setbacks.
It removes much of the defensiveness
that tends to occur in families.

RICHARD CARLSON

35
*Pray in the midst of your busiest days.
(Imagine that the Christ Child is
keeping you company.)*

On our busiest days, we often lose track of God. We allow our thoughts to be preoccupied with the business at hand; our emotions are swayed by circumstances; and we forget we are the beloved children of the King. Luckily for us, God doesn't lose track of us, no matter how busy we are. But when we lose our focus on Him, we also lose our sense of perspective, our peace, and our joy. We don't mean to. But we can't seem to prevent earthly distractions from clouding our vision.

But imagine that you are working on a pressing project while your toddler plays in the next room. All the while you are concentrating on the job at hand, another part of your mind is always listening for the sound of your child. In fact, as mothers of young children, we even listen in our sleep.

BALANCE FOR BUSY MOMS

We need to have the same listening heart when it comes to Christ. On busy days, we may have no time to shape a prayer—but we can still keep our hearts alert to God. Our love and attention can be constantly directed toward Him, no matter what other occupations fill our days. And isn't that what prayer really is?

Prayer continues in the desire of the heart
though the understanding be employed
on outward things.
In souls filled with love, the desire
to please God is a continual prayer.

JOHN WESLEY

Every encounter,
every incident during the day
is grist for the mill of the ongoing
God-human communication.
No activity is too small or too
unimportant to mediate the holy.

NORVENE VEST

36
Look for reminders in the structure of your day that will redirect your attention toward God.

If we had dedicated our lives to God five hundred years ago, we might have chosen to be cloistered in a convent where bells would have rung at regular intervals, calling us to prayer. As modern women, though, serving God in the midst of busy lives, God seldom rings any bells to get our attention. But we can still find ways to nudge our hearts awake.

Look at your day. What are the repeating patterns that structure the hours? Earlier in my life as a mother, nursing my babies was the recurring action that shaped my time. Today it might be coffee breaks, telephone calls, or the school bus. Whatever patterns you see in your own life, choose to see these as "bells," reminders that will call your heart to attention. Greet these moments with a heart consciously opened to God. You don't need to say a long and elaborate prayer. All you need to do is whisper a simple *I love You*—or even just His name.

Christ moves among the pots and pans.

TERESA OF AVILA

Help me, Lord, to remember that
religion is not to be confined
to the church or the closet,
nor exercised only in prayer
and meditation, but that
everywhere I am in thy Presence.

SUSANNA WESLEY

37
Forgive yourself when you drop a "ball."

We all drop "balls." Sometimes we do it more often than others, but sooner or later, all of us will forget something vital we were supposed to do, or we will neglect some responsibility we should be doing. But did we really think we were perfect?

If God dropped a ball, it really would be the end of the world. But we who are His creatures can relax in the knowledge that He will continue to hold our lives in His hands, no matter how many "balls" slip through our fingers.

Only God never makes a mistake. Stop expecting yourself to be God.

BALANCE FOR BUSY MOMS

Juggling, like any goal,
happens in time. . .[with] toleration
and persistence. Free from anxiety about
wild success or dismal failure,
your determination. . .can make it all
come together. . . . After a drop,
all you need to do is pick up the balls
and start throwing again.

STEVE COHEN

*A life spent making mistakes
is not only more honorable,
but more useful than
a life spent doing nothing.*

GEORGE BERNARD SHAW

38

Be patient with yourself.
Don't give up if it takes you months—
or even years—
to establish new routines.

Very few worthwhile things can be accomplished overnight. Keep your eyes on your goal rather than on your failures.

Desire is the key to motivation,
but it's your determination
and commitment to a goal—
your commitment to excellence—
that will enable you to
attain the success you seek.

MARIO ANDRETTI

Be patient. . .above all with thyself.
I mean, do not be disheartened
by your imperfections,
but always rise up with fresh courage.

FRANCIS DE SALES

≀≀

Knowing this,
that the trying of your faith
worketh patience.
But let patience have her perfect work,
that ye may be perfect and entire,
wanting nothing.

JAMES 1:3–4 KJV

39
Remember that God,
the Divine Juggler,
is your companion no matter what.

On the days when your juggling routine goes smoothly, when your job is on track, your family is happy, your home is ordered and serene, know that God is looking on you with favor, rejoicing in your contentment. And on the days when everything is falling apart, when your professional reputation is in question, your family is quarrelsome and unhappy, and your home is dusty and chaotic—God is still looking on you with favor. The Holy Juggler is your companion through all life's ups and downs. Nothing can separate you from His love. You do not juggle alone.

BALANCE FOR BUSY MOMS

Christ comes juggling our tombs,
tossing them high and higher yet,
until they hit the sun and break open
and we fall out, dancing and juggling
our griefs like sizzling balls of light.

EUGENE WARREN

ɜ͎͎ʃ

In all these things we are more than
conquerors through him who loved us.
For I am convinced that neither death
nor life, neither angels nor demons,
neither the present nor the future,
nor any powers, neither height nor depth,
nor anything else in all creation,
will be able to separate us from the love of
God that is in Christ Jesus our Lord.

ROMANS 8:37–39

40
Choose to be calm.
The crisis is seldom
as great as you think.

Some days everything seems like a catastrophe. My son confesses he's lost his shoes thirty seconds before the school bus comes. I spend my morning writing and then lose everything during a power failure. The raise we were counting on doesn't come through. The cat drags the kitchen garbage through the house. All these circumstances seem like overwhelming crises.

Sometimes I suspect we actually binge on adrenaline highs. Like Chicken Little, we dash around crying, "The sky is falling, the sky is falling!"—when if we just waited, we would find that the emergency was much smaller than we had thought—or even nonexistent. And yet we choose to live in a state of constant crisis.

Instead of turning everything into a catastrophe, we have another option—trust. Relaxed in

God's arms, we can rely on Him to work all things together for our good and His glory.

The first step in becoming
a more peaceful person
is to have the humility to
admit that, in most cases,
you're creating your own emergencies.
Life will usually go on if
things don't go according to plan.

RICHARD CARLSON

41
Let go of your anger.

Being angry takes energy. It's like weights tied to your hands, hampering your movement, slowing you down, making you tired and clumsy. You will find you have more to offer in other areas of your life once you let go of your anger—and you will be able to juggle far more smoothly without those heavy weights dragging on your hands.

Forgiving can be the beginning
of the healing process.
We must remember that hatred is like acid.
It does more damage to the vessel
in which it is stored than to the object
on which it is poured.

ANN LANDERS

42
Know when to ask for help.

Maybe it's pride that keeps me from admitting I can't do everything alone. Or maybe it's my need to be in control. Either way, I make my juggling routine harder for myself than it has to be.

The apostle Paul refers to the Body of Christ —all of us working together to help and support each other. We're not meant to do everything all by ourselves.

When life seems too much to handle—it's okay to ask for help.

In the face of an obstacle
which is impossible to overcome,
stubbornness is stupid.

SIMONE DE BEAUVIOR

43
Don't let others' expectations be your god.

When company's coming, I dash around the house, shining dust-dimmed surfaces, transforming cluttered countertops and hardwood floors into empty, gleaming expanses. I don't want anyone to suspect the slipshod way I often keep house. They might think less of me if they knew.

I worry about others' opinions in other areas of my life as well. I long to please; I hate to disappoint. I try to be just what others want.

I'm not the only woman who does this, either. Many of us were trained to be good little girls, sweet and compliant and eager to please. We know in our hearts we'll never live up to the expectations of others—but we still try as hard as we can. In fact, we try so hard, we exhaust ourselves. The expectations of others becomes an enormous "ball" we strain to juggle.

Recently, though, I realized that when I live my life this way, I'm turning others' expectations into my god. I'm struggling so hard to keep this ponderous, impossibly heavy "ball" up in the air that I have no energy left for some of the joyous activities God longs for me to experience.

And yet all of us sometimes worship at the feet of this false god. We may have done it so long we don't even realize what we're doing; we've forgotten we have a choice. But we don't need to worship at the god of others' expectations anymore. Jesus came to set us free to be ourselves, without shame or embarrassment. He wants to take this bowling ball-sized burden from us and replace it with His grace.

You must worship no other gods,
but only the Lord,
for he is a God who is passionate about
his relationship with you.

EXODUS 34:14 NLT

*No one can make you feel inferior
without your consent.*

ELEANOR ROOSEVELT

~}/

Don't copy the behavior
and customs of this world,
but be a new and different person
with a fresh newness
in all you do and think.

ROMANS 12:2 TLB

44
Honor the Sabbath. Set aside time in your schedule for doing nothing.

In today's Christian culture, we've come to equate the Sabbath with church functions. Certainly, gathering together to worship and learn about God is one good way to use our Sabbath time. But sometimes we become so busy with church responsibilities, that our Sundays are as exhausting as any other day. When we do that, we've lost sight of the real meaning of the word "Sabbath."

"Sabbath" means simply *rest*. God designed the Sabbath to be a time of holy leisure—a time to relax and enjoy His presence, to restore our bodies, our hearts, and our minds. If your Sundays are a busy cycle of church and company dinners and then church again, you may need to find Sabbath time somewhere else in your week.

We're so accustomed to being busy. We feel

guilty if we stop all the juggling and simply rest. We believe that every moment of our time has to be productive.

But the Old Testament also uses the word "Sabbath" to refer to fields that are allowed to lie fallow, with no crops, producing nothing. The early Hebrews understood that the soil's fertile life can be exhausted; the fields that are allowed to rest will later produce the richest crops.

We are the same as those fields. Sabbath time is not wasted time. During these quiet, restful moments, God renews our spirits.

He makes me lie down
in green pastures,
he leads me beside quiet waters,
he restores my soul.

PSALM 23:2–3

How beautiful it is to do nothing,
and then rest afterward.

SPANISH PROVERB

45
If possible, schedule a few "sabbath" moments every day.

When my children take swimming lessons each summer, they swim in the large school pool while I watch with the other parents from the other side of a wall of windows. Most of the time the groups of children are too involved with splashing and jumping and paddling to notice the loving audience that watches them from the other side of the glass. But every now and then, each child turns and looks for the one face that matters.

When I see one of my children search for me, I hold up my hand—my thumb, forefinger, and little finger raised, my two middle fingers down: the "I love you" sign. I see my child's face light up, and then she goes back to swimming—splashing harder, leaping straighter, knowing that I'm watching.

God, too, is a loving Parent, waiting for a

chance to show His children His love. If we don't turn and look for His face, though, we'll miss Him. We need to schedule small moments in our day when we can turn and see the "I love you" signs He's sending our way. These are moments of quiet and rest, small sabbaths that can happen even in the busiest days.

Scheduling a little time each day as if it were an actual appointment may be the only way you can ensure you will keep this tiny appointment with God. You might become an early riser, for example, and schedule an hour or a half an hour every morning, a quiet time you reserve for reading, praying, reflecting. You might turn off the television a half hour earlier at night and find a few sabbath moments before you go to bed as you sip a cup of tea and listen to your favorite music. Or you might take a walk alone after supper—or simply sit at your desk for a few moments in the middle of the day with a cup of coffee in your hand and your eyes on your Father. The important thing is that you schedule these moments every day.

*Let us do our best to
enter that place of rest.*

HEBREWS 4:11 NLT

Work is not always required. . .
there is such a thing as sacred idleness,
the cultivation of which is
now fearfully neglected.

GEORGE MACDONALD

46
On your most frantic days, take time for "sabbath time" alone with God.

When a busy day lies ahead, we may be tempted to skip the small moments of relaxation we usually include in our routines. *I just don't have time today,* we tell ourselves. We'd feel guilty if we weren't "on task" every moment of the upcoming day.

But really, we need those quiet times even more when we are stressed and pressured than we do on our calm and serene days. Taking a half hour to restore our souls will help us manage the rest of our busy hours more efficiently. We will be more physically alert, more emotionally balanced, and more spiritually creative because of those moments spent with God.

*If women were convinced that. . .
an hour of solitude was
a reasonable ambition,
they would find a way of attaining it.
As it is,
they feel so unjustified in their
demand
that they rarely make the attempt.*

ANNE MORROW LINDBERGH

47
Be realistic about how many "balls" you can juggle at once.

Time-management books are best-sellers these days. We're all hoping that someone will have the magic answer to our lives. Someone out there will be able to tell us how to do it all—be good parents, pursue our professions, manage our homes, be active in our churches and communities. . . If we were just more efficient, if someone would just teach us their secret time-management tricks, we might be able to keep the countless balls we juggle spinning flawlessly and tranquilly above our heads.

But that's a fantasy. As human beings, we all have limitations. Time itself is limited. So no matter how skillful you are at juggling, there is an optimum number of "balls" you can handle at once. No one can do it all.

Ask God to show you how many activities He wants you to be juggling at this point in your life. And then be willing to put a "ball" or two down.

One who begins too much accomplishes little.

GERMAN PROVERB

〉〉〉

Juggling Tip:

In her book *Time Management from the Inside Out*, professional organizer Julie Morgenstern recommends that you ask yourself two questions before you take on any new activity:

- Does this task fit in with my chosen activities?
- How long will this take me to do?

48
Allow adequate time for each "ball" you juggle.

I'm not always realistic about how much I can do during the day—and then I'm frustrated and disappointed and guilty when bedtime comes. I feel like I should have accomplished more. But when I sit down and assess the hours or minutes I truly need for each task—and then compare that to the hours in my day—I'm surprised to find I'd need a forty-hour day to get to everything on my daily to-do list.

I manage my time far more effectively when my daily plans are more realistic. If time is the container into which I place my life's activities, I need to understand the actual dimensions of that container, as well as the size of the individual tasks I place inside it. Otherwise, I'm like a child who thinks she can put her doll, her toy truck, and her books all in a matchbox.

*A prudent man foresees
the difficulties ahead
and prepares for them.*

PROVERBS 22:3 TLB

~ξ~

Just as a closet is a limited space into which you must fit a certain number of objects, a schedule is a limited space into which you must fit a certain number of tasks.

Your days are not infinite and endless.

JULIE MORGENSTERN

~ξ~

Time factors you may forget to include as you plan your day:

- setup time
- time to think

- time consumed by mistakes
- cleanup time
- travel time
- "sabbath" time (time to pause for refreshment—physically, emotionally, and spiritually)

49
Practice saying no.

As women, most of us long to please those we love. And then there's that demanding little god we talked about earlier—the god of others' expectations. These two factors in our makeup often lead to us picking up more "balls" than we can handle. Whenever anyone approaches us with a new request, we always say yes.

But if we want to limit the number of activities we juggle, we are going to have to say no to something. If you find the word "yes" coming out of your mouth automatically, practice ways to say no ahead of time. Here are some suggestions:

- "Thank you for thinking of me. Unfortunately, I can't make it." (You really don't need to explain why.)
- "That sounds like a wonderful project. But I won't be able to fit it into

my schedule right now."

- "I have a previous engagement."
  (Appointments to spend time with
  God, your husband, or even your-
  self are all legitimate "engage-
  ments." You do not need to feel
  you should elaborate.)
- "Someone else needs to do that."
- "I'm sorry, but I just can't."
- "No, thank you."
- "No."

*We're swallowed up only when
we are willing for it to happen.*

NATHALIE SARRAUTE

Saying "no" can be the ultimate self-care.

CLAUDIA BLACK

50
Give God your "guilt ball."

If I'm working on a writing project, I often feel sorry I'm not spending time with my kids. But if I am spending time with my children, I feel anxious because I'm not getting any writing accomplished. While I research a project on the Internet, piles of dirty laundry nag at my thoughts. But if I leave my computer and go tackle the laundry, I feel guilty that I'm not devoting myself to my professional work. Whatever I'm doing, I always should be doing something else as well. These mental habits are obviously silly and nonproductive, but many women I know have similar feelings.

How can we have the energy and coordination we need to juggle our lives when we're carrying such a heavy load of guilt? This sort of guilt is neither healthy nor productive. And it is not God's voice we are listening to; His Spirit does not accuse us of doing too little when we are already doing the best we can.

Imagine your guilt as a lumpy ugly ball you've been struggling to include in your juggling routine. This ball is so heavy, so rough and sharp, that it wounds your hands each time you touch it; you're exhausted from trying to keep it up in the air. So take that ball—and put it in Christ's scarred hands.

Despite how heavy this ball is, you'll find it has an amazing ability to bounce back into your hands. When it does, as many times a day as you need to, simply give it back to Jesus.

My tidiness and my untidiness are full of regret and remorse and complex feelings.

NATALIE GINSBERG

૨૪૪

For the Accuser has been thrown down
    to earth—
the one who accused our brothers and
    sisters before our God day and night.
And they have defeated him because of
    the blood of the Lamb. . . .

REVELATION 12:10–11 NLT

51
Take time to acknowledge your feelings.

We sometimes forget that we also juggle emotions. We may try to ignore our sadness or loneliness or frustration on any given day; we assume we simply don't have time for our feelings, and so we try to push them aside. We should maintain a calm exterior, we tell ourselves; as adult women, we cannot afford to live at the mercy of our emotions.

But feelings do not go away so conveniently. Instead, as we reach for a "family ball," we may find ourselves grasping our frustration by mistake—or anger and depression may come spilling out just when we're trying to deal with a "professional ball."

We will manage our time far more smoothly if we acknowledge the emotional balls we're juggling as well on any given day. When we consider how much we can fit into a day, our emotions need to be taken into consideration as well; obviously, when we're happy and calm we can handle far more than when we are overwhelmed with despair.

Make allowances for your emotions. Set aside time to talk them over with a friend. If they're too overwhelming, consider scheduling an appointment with your pastor or a counselor. And ask God for His help as you juggle your emotions.

*For years I have endeavored
to calm an impetuous tide—
laboring to make my feelings
take an orderly course—
it was striving against the stream.*

MARY WOLLSTONECRAFT

52
Let go of your need to be needed.

As women, most of us like to be needed. Maybe it soothes our own insecurities. Or maybe we are simply warmed by being able to give to those we love.

But our need to be needed can become another of those false gods we fall down and worship. Serving this god, we may miss those activities to which God is truly calling us. We will often neglect ourselves and fail to become the people God created us to be.

Don't let your need to be needed control your life. Serve the one true God instead.

Long term change requires looking honestly at our lives and realizing that it's nice to be needed, but not at the expense of our health, our happiness, and our sanity.

ELLEN SUE STERN

53
Let God take care of those "balls"
on which you can't focus until later.

We can't do everything at once. Sometimes we have to set some "balls" down while we concentrate on other aspects of our lives. I think this is particularly hard for us as mothers when we have to focus on something other than our children for a portion of our day. It's not just that we feel guilty about leaving them—our hearts also long to be with them. We worry about their well-being if we're not watching over them; we miss the warmth of their closeness.

But we can rely on God to be with our children when we can't be. He uses us as mothers to nurture and care for our children—but He will continue to nurture and care for them even when we are not present. He will never leave them.

*At work, you think of the children
you have left at home.
At home, you think of the work
you've left unfinished.
Such a struggle is unleashed
within yourself.
Your heart is rent.*

GOLDA MEIR

54
Accept your limitations.

All of us have unique talents and strengths—and we all have our own individual weaknesses as well. For instance, I am good with words—but I can't hit a tennis ball. I've even disproved the old maxim that says no one ever forgets how to ride a bicycle—when I got on my teenage daughter's bike last night, I found I didn't remember how to balance.

I've never been physically coordinated. As a kid, my clumsiness filled me with embarrassment and shame. As an adult, those old feelings of insecurity can sometimes wash over me. But I find I'm learning to enjoy physical activity simply for the exercise. Now that gym class is no longer a dreaded reality in my life, what difference does it make if I can never hit a softball or turn a cartwheel?

None of us is good at everything. Once we accept that, we are free to concentrate on the things we do well. If you're struggling to juggle some activity that lies outside your skills, if you've given it a chance and you're still not getting the knack of it—maybe it's time to set this particular "ball" down.

To dream of the person you would like to be is to waste the person you are.

ANONYMOUS

ۅۅۅ

I think knowing what you cannot do is more important than knowing what you can do.

LUCILLE BALL

55
Think positively.
Worry wastes your energy.

Looking back at my life, I realize I wasted hour upon hour worrying about things that never even happened. Even on those few occasions when the bad things I anticipated did in fact happen, my hours of worrying didn't make me any better able to handle the crisis when it came. All those hours could have been used far more effectively.

It's a waste of time to juggle the "worry ball."

I think these difficult times
have helped me to understand
better than before how infinitely rich
and beautiful life is in every way
and that so many things that one goes
around worrying aboutare of
no importance whatsoever.

ISAK DINESON

I realize what a lot of negativity there is
in the world and all around us,
and how easy it is to become a part
of that negativity and to be sucked into it
and become part of the chaos and confusion
if one isn't very careful.

EILEEN CADY

کہ

Who of you by worrying can add a
single hour to his life?
Since you cannot do this very little
thing, why do you worry about the
rest?
Do not be afraid. . .for your Father
has been pleased to give you the
kingdom.

JESUS OF NAZARETH (LUKE 12:25–26, 32)

56
If possible,
focus on one ball at a time.

Many times our attention is so divided between our responsibilities that we never give ourselves wholeheartedly to any task. But if we focus on the one thing we're doing now, letting the rest drop out of our consciousness into God's hands, we will find ourselves truly living in the present moment, that tiny space that touches Eternity. With our minds focused, not scattered between five different responsibilities, we often find we can accomplish far more in a shorter period.

Being a "good mother"
does not call for the same qualities
as being a "good" housewife,
and the pressure to be both at the same time
may be an insupportable burden.

ANN OAKLEY

57
When focusing on one single ball is impossible, learn to "multitask."

As I've studied different time-management authorities, I was interested to note that male authors were more apt to insist we should do one thing at a time, while women authors tended to favor "multitasking." Ideally, I suspect that giving ourselves totally to the task at hand would be the best way to live our lives. But as mothers, we simply don't always have that luxury. Children do not conveniently disappear while we cook supper or clean the house. And our days are so filled with countless tasks that we would never get to them all if we didn't double them up sometimes.

The fact is, many tasks can be done at the same time. This is one juggling trick that will help us fit more into our days. Like most things in life, though, too much of a good thing can become a bad thing. We should use this technique in moderation.

It's not necessary to do
just one thing at a time until it's done.
This can be a real creativity stunter.
We need to take advantage of
our multilayer brains.

LEE SILBER

Activities that can be done at the same time:

- talk on the phone and clean your kitchen or fold the laundry
- exercise and read a book or listen to a tape
- clean the kitchen and help your child prepare for a test
- watch television and pay bills
- supervise your child's homework and sort the mail
- drive and do stomach exercises
- cook and clean as you work
- pray while you do almost anything
- exercise and get together with a friend

58
Try not to juggle other people's lives for them.

When we have so many balls of our own to juggle, why is that we try to take on other people's juggling routines as well? This is particularly tempting with our children. Obviously, young children cannot juggle their lives by themselves, but as our kids grow older, they are perfectly capable of developing this skill for themselves. Instead, though, we may find ourselves so involved with their homework projects, their after-school activities, and their busy social lives that we have little energy left over for our own lives. Preoccupied with our children's schedules, we lose track of our own.

Our children will continue to need our guidance as they grow older. And our friends may want and respect our advice. But ultimately, we're not doing anyone any favors if we try to juggle their lives for them. And we may miss out on what God wants for us instead.

The true secret of giving advice is,
after you have honestly given it,
to be perfectly indifferent
whether it is taken or not
and never persist in trying to
set people right.

HANNAH WHITALL SMITH

59
Pay attention to the details.

Sometimes we're so focused on our larger goals that we're impatient with all the tedious small responsibilities we juggle. But whatever goal you have—whether it's a clean house, a professional achievement, or a well-balanced child—you'll never accomplish it if you ignore the little tasks along the way. Those details may seem trivial and insignificant—but a house will never shine if you don't dust the corners, wash the table and counters, and pick up the myriad pieces of paper that seem to multiply everywhere; a professional achievement will never be realized without dedicated attention to countless small, seemingly unimportant tasks; and a child will never grow strong and whole without reading him hundreds of stories, supervising thousands of meals and baths and bedtimes, and hugging and kissing him about a million times. Each tiny detail is an essential and significant ingredient in the great shining goal you are working toward.

*I long to accomplish
a great and noble task,
but it is my chief duty to accomplish
small tasks as if they
were great and noble.*

HELEN KELLER

❧

Great things are not done by impulse,
but by a series of small things
brought together.

VINCENT VAN GOGH

60
Make your daily routines as simple as possible. (Some details are unnecessary.)

Do you really need to go to the grocery store five times a week? Or might you streamline your life if you organized your shopping list on a weekly basis?

Is it necessary to do a blue load of laundry, a red load, a purple load, a black load, and a white load? Or if you allowed your children to simply sort the clothes into colored clothes and light, would they be able to take over some of the laundry responsibilities?

Do you need to save every picture your child creates? Or could you ask her to sort out one favorite for you to display at regular intervals?

Sometimes we do something a certain way merely because we've always done it that way. For instance, when I first got married, I realized I was washing my dishes in the left sink, then rinsing them in the right, and then placing them to my left to drain, simply because my mother always washed her dishes from left to right. My mother, though, had room on the right end of her counter for a dish drainer, while I didn't. It finally occurred to me that no rule said I had to wash my dishes from left to right. Since my drainer was on the left, I could choose to wash from right to left, which would be far more convenient.

If you look at your life closely, you may be surprised to find you too have unnecessary routines. Try to dispense with the unnecessary details. When you do, you'll find you have more time for other activities.

Our life is frittered away by detail. . .
Simplify. Simplify.

HENRY DAVID THOREAU

61
Sort the clutter out of your life.

Each year when we go on vacation to a cottage, I'm always surprised and delighted by how easily we get by with only a suitcase of belongings for each of us. The children's rooms stay far neater, the living room never gets messy and chaotic, and the laundry chores seem more manageable. I realize then how much of my life I spend picking up and cleaning my family's possessions. If we had fewer belongings, my chores would be shorter.

So the question is—if we can get along for two weeks without all that stuff, do we really need it the rest of the time?

Have nothing in your house that
you do not know to be useful
or believe to be beautiful.

WILLIAM MORRIS

Out of clutter, find simplicity.

ALBERT EINSTEIN

≀≀≀

Hints for reducing clutter:

- Whenever possible, each time you bring something new into the house (whether a new toy, an item of clothing, a knickknack, a dish, a piece of bedding, or new shoes), discard an old item from your household. (Recycle it if it's worn out, or give it to charity if someone else could use it.) Developing this habit prevents clutter from accumulating.
- Cancel subscriptions if you rarely read the magazines. Recycle or donate old issues.
- Go through your family's closets. If an item of clothing hasn't been worn for more than a year, donate it to charity.
- According to professional organizers, most people only use about 20

percent of their belongings. That means the other 80 percent is pretty much clutter. To determine the 20 percent you need to keep, pretend that a fire or flood threatens your home. You have 30 minutes to remove whatever is most important to you. What would you take? Consider getting rid of the rest.

62
Think twice before you make any purchase.

One good way to decrease the amount of clutter in your house is to stop buying so many things. Impulse purchases only add to the amount of stuff you will have to organize, pick up, and keep clean. Before you buy anything, ask yourself, Do I really need this?

*One day I had
the sudden realization:
If I stopped buying things
right this moment,
there is no way I could
use all I have now.*

DON ASLETT

63
Make friends with Time.

Sometimes I see Time as an ogre. Time sneaks up behind me and grabs things out of my grasp; Time demands that I submit to its relentless authority. "Time's up!" it shouts. *But wait,* I want to say; *I'm not done yet.* But it's too late; time marches on, limiting my chances. The tick-tick-tick of its passage gobbles up my reality second by second, devouring my life, stealing things from me before I'm ready to part with them.

Our culture often looks at Time this way, as though it were a cruel enemy to be battled. But in reality, just as Time takes things away from us, Time also brings us new gifts. From one perspective, Time may look like a threatening monster crouching behind us—but if you turn around, Time may wear the smiling face of a pregnant mother, ready to reveal her newest child. It all depends on your perspective.

Like the rest of our world, Time is a creation

of God. He never intended for us to fear it. Instead, He means for us to enjoy Time. It is His gift to us.

*The secret of life is
enjoying the passage of time.*

JAMES TAYLOR

64
Put people first.

A work deadline, a messy house, or a church commitment may all seem like more pressing responsibilities then a worried child, a friend who needs to talk, or lonely elderly parents. But when we find the people in our lives being pushed aside by the other "balls" we juggle, we need to reevaluate our priorities. Earthly achievements are only temporary—but our relationships with those we love will last for Eternity.

At the end of your life,
you will never regret not having
passed one more test,
not winning one more verdict
or not closing one more deal.
You will regret time not spent with a husband,
a friend, a child or a parent.

BARBARA BUSH

One way to ensure that you make time for the most important people in your life—your family—each and every day is to create family rituals. When these become an established pattern of action, they require less energy and planning. Here are some examples:

- Make one night a week "Family Night"—probably a Friday, Saturday, or Sunday. You can do anything you want that evening—go out to eat, play games, watch a video, go on a camp out, go for a walk around the neighborhood—but you have to do it as a family. If someone asks you if you're free to do something else on that particular night of the week, make a habit of saying, "I'm sorry. I already have a commitment."
- Spend a few minutes alone with each child at bedtime. This is a good time for prayer and quiet talk about the day's events.
- Try to eat dinner as a family.
- Read books aloud as a family.
- Plan a weekly meal or baking project that involves the entire family.

- Make weekend chores a family
  event. Then reward yourselves afterward with a family "treat."

65
Choose not to
answer the phone sometimes.

The telephone has become a household god. When this god demands attention, we leap to answer it. We allow it to interrupt our sleep, our conversations, and our concentration. We behave as though its voice were the number-one priority in our lives.

With the growing popularity of cell phones, this god now reaches us with its greedy grasp even beyond the walls of our homes. There is nowhere we are safe from its demands; it summons us when we are driving, while we are eating out with friends, and while we are shopping.

I believe the telephone is a wonderful invention, and the cell phone is a convenience I depend on as well. But the telephone should be just that—a convenience, something that makes our lives easier—rather than a demanding god who interrupts our juggling routines for the most trivial reasons. Ask God to help you use your telephone wisely.

The reason the computer can do work faster than a human being is that it doesn't have to answer the phone.

UNKNOWN

}}}

Simple as it seems,
choosing not to answer the phone,
on selected occasions,
can be a very empowering decision
and can greatly reduce the stress
in your home life.

RICHARD CARLSON

66
Make sure you get enough rest.

I often ignore my body's needs—and the busier I am, the more likely I am to cheat my body of the sleep it requires. I act as though sleep were an optional activity.

The reality is far different. The busier our lives are, the more crowded and rushed our juggling routines, the more we need to ensure we have adequate rest. In fact, many researchers are now reporting that most Americans are sleep deprived. As a result, we function far less effectively both at work and at home.

Most adults need seven to nine hours of sleep each night. If necessary, schedule your bedtime on your weekly planner. But don't neglect your body's need for rest. Remember—your body is the Spirit's temple. Sleep is one way we keep that temple strong and whole.

Sometimes it is hard to admit
that overwork is sin, but it is.
Overwork is destructive of
the temple of the Holy Spirit.
It dims the vision,
sharpens the temper,
kills creativity, and deadens
spiritual sensitivity.

M. HELLENE POLLOCK

For the love of God,
look at things from another point of view,
and stop devoting the hours
you ought to be asleep
to either making plans—
or even to prayer.

TERESA OF AVILA

67
Exercise.

Sometimes I behave as though my body were a tool that could serve me endlessly without my investing in its maintenance. Just as I often ignore my need for sleep, I've also ignored my body's need for exercise. And yet as I've established a regular exercise routine, I find that I'm able to juggle the rest of my life with more energy and stamina.

Until this year, exercising was the first thing I would drop from my life when my juggling routine became more rushed. On a busy day when I was scrambling to meet a deadline, spending a half an hour exercising seemed like something I could easily do without. However, that one busy day would generally turn into a week and then a month—until eventually, I would realize with a sense of discouragement that I had once again allowed the "exercise ball" to roll off into some far, dark corner.

This year, though, I reexamined my priorities. I realized that as much as I wanted to be fit and strong, my priority was always focused on outside accomplishments. And yet eventually, as I grow older, those accomplishments will no longer be possible if I've failed to care for my body.

Lately, I've begun to compare exercising to taking a shower. No matter how busy my day, I always wash myself. That's because cleanliness is a priority I wouldn't consider doing without. I'm coming to see the half hour I spend exercising as the same sort of given in my day's routine. That half hour will not cost me much in terms of my daily accomplishment—and it may yield me years' worth of potential achievement.

I don't have time to not exercise.

RICHARD CARLSON

Ways to include more exercise in your life:

- Walk instead of drive whenever you can.

BALANCE FOR BUSY MOMS

- Climb the stairs instead of taking the elevator.
- Make a practice of parking as far from your ultimate destination as you can.
- Play active games with your kids.
- When a friend wants to get together, suggest a walk date rather than meeting over a table.
- Walk during your lunch hour.

68
Organize your belongings.

If you're like me, your keys have a habit of landing in the oddest places; your children's shoes have the ability to walk off into strange corners all on their own; and the particular bill you need to pay right now is always buried under a pile of your children's school papers. I hate to think how much time I waste looking for items I can't find.

I discovered that the American Demographics Society had already figured it out for me. According to this research group, Americans as a group waste nine million hours per day searching for misplaced items. The *Wall Street Journal* reports that the average American executive wastes six weeks per year (one hour a day) searching for missing information in messy offices.

Just think how much time you and I could save if we knew where all our belongings were.

It is not enough if you are busy.
The question is,
What are you busy about?

HENRY DAVID THOREAU

69
Break big jobs down into smaller pieces.

When we face certain demands on our time—for instance, a messy house, a demanding work project, or a long-standing family problem—we may be so overwhelmed by the sheer enormity of the job that we hate to even begin. That's why we need to break the activity down into smaller, more manageable pieces.

Teachers do this all the time when they teach their students new skills. For instance, they begin with the ABCs rather than Shakespeare. "A is for apple" may seem to have very little to do with "Is this a dagger I see before me, the handle toward my hand"—but none of us would ever be able to read *Macbeth* if someone hadn't first, long ago, taught us about As and apples, giving us that first small bite of knowledge.

In the same way, cleaning your kitchen counter may seem like such a small job compared to all that needs to be done in your house.

But that countertop is a nonthreatening task you can accomplish today. And when that's done, tomorrow you can go on to another small job, and then another, until little by little your home becomes ordered once more.

If a particular chore is
too complex and cumbersome,
chances are you'll avoid it altogether.

JULIE MORGENSTERN

70
Learn to delegate.

Our need for control, our need to be needed, our need to do everything perfectly—all these things lead us to believe that we have to do everything ourselves. As mothers, though, our juggling routines will be far less stressful if we begin to share the workload with the other members of our families. Even the youngest children can participate.

Chores for preschoolers:

- Put dirty laundry in the washing machine. (They may need to stand on a chair if you have a top loader.)
- Set the table.
- Bring the waste paper baskets from around the house on the evening before garbage pickup.
- Water plants (with supervision!).

- Clear their places from the table.
- Pick up toys.

Chores for grade school children:

- Sort the recycling.
- Empty the dishwasher.
- Make their beds.
- Keep their rooms clean.
- Sort laundry.
- Put their folded laundry away.

Chores for teenagers:

- Be responsible for their own laundry.
- Prepare meals.
- Vacuum.
- Shovel snow.
- Wash the car.
- Make school lunches.

71
Allow time for creativity.

Creativity is an activity that refuses to conform to a time schedule. We can't write on our daily planner between 9:00 and 10:00 A.M., "have a wonderful idea" or "create a masterpiece" or "express myself in a fresh new way." Creativity just doesn't work that way. It's an elusive thing that slips away between the harsh demands of appointments and deadlines. Instead, creativity blossoms when we least expect it, when our minds are focused on some other ordinary occupation—like raking the leaves or taking a walk or simply sitting beside a stream doing nothing at all.

You may think you have little use for creativity in your daily life—but no matter what activities fill your hours, we all need new insights, fresh slants on life, and startling glimpses of something that just might work. We need to allow for these unpredictable, unscheduled mental leaps by taking time for stillness and reflection.

After all, human creativity is one way God shows us His face.

Women's normal occupations
in general
run counter to creative life. . . .

ANNE MORROW LINDBERGH

72
Handle each piece of mail only once.

We all know that the phone can be a demanding god—but I suspect the postal service is nearly as bad. (Imagine the world two hundred years ago, when the phone never rang and letters were rare and treasured; just think of how much you and I might have accomplished back then!)

One way to control this small god's power is to handle each piece of mail only once. Instead of allowing piles of paper to accumulate on our countertops and desks, we can choose to form the habit of sorting the mail as it arrives, tossing some into the recycling bin and responding immediately to bills and other pieces of mail that require an answer. This saves us from the overwhelming task of sorting through weeks' worth of accumulated mail. And it also reduces the likelihood that we'll waste precious minutes (or hours!) searching for that lost bill or insurance form.

Researchers tell us that it takes three weeks to establish a new habit. That means you have to make a conscious effort to practice a new behavior every day for twenty-one days in a row.

Time is the coin of your life.
It is the only coin you have,
and only you can determine
how it will be spent.
Be careful lest you let
other people spend it for you.

CARL SANDBURG

$\mathcal{O}ur$ culture tells us our work products are the concrete symbols of our personal worth. As mothers, then, it's no wonder we often find ourselves feeling frustrated, discouraged, and resentful. We make a bed in the morning, only to have it unmade that night; we dust the furniture only to have it need dusting after a few days' time; and then there's the family laundry, a chore that's apparently as endless as the universe. On cleaning days I sometimes feel as though my children follow happily behind me, messing up the house more quickly than I can clean it. When my husband's eyebrows rise as the level of my desperation and impatience climbs, I turn on him and demand, "How would you like it if the children went in your office at work and scribbled on the report you had just finished? Would you just smile sweetly and start all over again?"

No, he wouldn't smile—and neither do I. Obviously, my ego is invested in my work. I'm thirsty for success; I want others to recognize my achievement.

When we let go of our pride, we may find we can look at our work with new eyes.

The trouble with being in the rat race is that even if you win, you're still a rat.

LILY TOMLIN

We ought not to be weary of doing little things for the love of God, who regards not the greatness of the work, but the love with which it is performed.

BROTHER LAWRENCE

74
Focus on the process rather than the end result.

Once we let go of our achievement-oriented approach to work, we may find we can focus instead on the process itself, rather than the end result. When we do that, repetitive, even monotonous acts—like making a bed or sweeping the floor—can become vehicles for reflection and prayer, quiet moments when God's grace can touch our hearts.

Happiness is not a destination.
It is the attitude with which
you choose to travel.

ARIT DESAL

75
Ask for God's help.

We often choose to juggle our lives in our own strength rather than depending on God's. Despite our faith, we cannot help but be influenced by the prevailing viewpoint, the worldview that assumes only those things we can see and touch are real. From this perspective, God's grace is an intangible, impractical thing on which to rely.

But grace is woven through the very fabric of the universe. God's love and power keep the Milky Way whirling in its place—and He is able to infuse our small juggling routines with the same joyful rhythm. All we need to do is rely on His strength rather than our own.

While they are still talking
to me about their needs,
I will go ahead and answer their prayers!

ISAIAH 65:24 NLT

76
Give your body the nourishment it needs.

Our bodies cannot function without fuel. Skipping meals on a busy day makes as much sense as refusing to put gasoline in our cars before a long trip.

Here are some ways to nourish your body well:

- Choose low-fat versions of foods—but watch that the sugar content in these foods isn't raised.
- Eat foods in their natural state—rather than cooked, canned, or processed—as often as possible. Their vitamin and fiber contents will be higher.
- When you eat carbohydrates, choose whole grains over processed white flour. The increased fiber content

means they will be turned into sugar less quickly—and your body actually expends some calories digesting them. Besides, your digestive tract needs fiber to stay healthy.

- Eat 3–5 servings of vegetables and 2–4 servings of fruit every day.
- Minimize the sugars and fats in your diets.
- Consume adequate calories. Calories are your body's fuel; you will not be able to juggle smoothly if you are literally running on empty. Even if you are dieting, do not starve yourself. Research has proven that in the long run, extreme diets don't work; the most effective weight-loss programs are based on a sensible diet and exercise.

*He shall feed his flock
like a shepherd.*

ISAIAH 40:11 KJV

77
Resist the temptation of distractions.

Temptations pull us off the road we have chosen. Like spoiled adolescents demanding instant gratification, we lose sight of our ultimate goal and opt for what feels good right now. But many of our desires are fleeting; if we waited, if we considered the larger picture, we would see that resisting these temporary desires actually leads us back to our truest heart's desires.

It may seem easier, more desirable, more pleasant to fall back into our old nonproductive time-management habits. But we usually find all over again that those habits are self-destructive.

Life is made up of desires that
seem big and vital one minute,
and little and absurd the next.

ALICE CALDWELL RICE

78
Let the past go.
Don't waste your energy on yesterday's mistakes.

At the church my family attends, we often pray these words together: "I have sinned through my own fault, in my thoughts and in my words, in what I have done, and in what I have failed to do." We pray these words as a congregation, because we recognize that we have all dropped "balls." By doing so, we have failed our loved ones and embarrassed ourselves. Most of all, we have failed God.

But we lose our focus and waste energy when we dwell too much on yesterday's mistakes. What's more, by doing so we miss out on the grace and power God wants to give us now. He will not only forgive the mistakes we have made, but when we surrender them to Him, He will even—somehow—use them for the glory of His kingdom.

BALANCE FOR BUSY MOMS

We can never undo the past. All we can do is trust God. Once we do, we are free to turn our eyes back to the central focus of these lives we juggle—the vision to which God is calling us.

Finish every day and be done with it.
You have done what you could.

RALPH WALDO EMERSON

Let us not go over the old ground,
let us rather prepare for what is to come.

CICERO

79
Make use of times when you are forced to wait during your day.

Carry a notepad, stationery, or your journal in your bag. Then you can use the time you wait in doctors' and dentists' offices to make plans, write letters, and reflect. Or carry a book with you and catch up on your reading. Listen to tapes or pray when you're in the car alone— and when family members accompany you, use the drive to catch up with each other. Even small periods of time, like when you're waiting in line at the grocery store or post office, can become moments of prayer, a tiny space where you come into God's presence.

*Time is what we want most
but what we use worst.*

WILLIAM PENN

80

Try going to bed thirty minutes earlier and getting up thirty minutes earlier.

The last thirty minutes before we go to bed are seldom the most productive. We can usually snip this half hour off the day without even missing it.

But when we add this extra half hour to our mornings, we often gain a quiet space, thirty silent moments when we will not be interrupted by the phone or our children. We can use this time to:

- Pray.
- Exercise.
- Write in a journal.
- Review the day's juggling routine.
- Prepare for the day ahead.

Just half an hour can help us juggle far more easily.

Yesterday is a canceled check;
Tomorrow is a promissory note;
Today is cash in hand:
Spend it wisely.

ANONYMOUS

81
Whenever possible, communicate by E-mail, voice mail, or letter.

Face it—talking to people takes time. We need to make the time to communicate often with those who matter most to us—but we don't need to have daily heart-to-hearts with the receptionist at our doctor's office, the insurance representative, or each and every one of our work colleagues. Communicating by E-mail, voice mail, or letter saves time we can use for that which is most essential in our lives.

Anything less than a
conscious commitment to the important
is an unconscious commitment to
the unimportant.

STEPHEN COVEY

82
Drink at least eight glasses of water a day.

Having a glass of water doesn't seem to have much to do with managing our time more efficiently. That's because our culture divides our minds and our bodies into two neatly separated sections. We act as though we can ignore our bodies' needs, and still expect peak performance from ourselves as we rush through our busy days. The busier we are, the more we tend to forget about taking care of our bodies.

In fact, though, just the opposite should be true: The busier we are, the more stress we are expecting our bodies to handle—and the more we need to be sure we are giving them what they need. Water helps our vital organs—including our brains—do their jobs more efficiently. Research shows that when we fail to drink enough, we often find ourselves feeling tired, weak, and listless; we may experience sore muscles, nervousness, and even depression.

Giving our bodies all the water they need is a pretty small "ball" to juggle. If we add this habit to our routine, we will need only a few extra minutes out of every day—but the rewards may surprise us. We will find ourselves able to juggle much more smoothly when our bodies are not crying out for the water they need.

So whatever kind of day you have planned, carry a water bottle with you—and drink up!

*Then God opened her eyes
and she saw a well of water.*

GENESIS 21:19

83
Turn off your television.

Earlier I talked about the household "gods" we worship—the telephone and the mail. But there's another god that is still more imperious. As families, we gather around this god's throne and stare fixedly. Worshipping on a nightly basis, we allow this god to consume huge quantities of our time.

I don't believe television is inherently evil. It can offer our families education and amusement and moments of family togetherness. But most of us need to break the habit of automatically turning on the television whenever we have an hour or two of relaxation. These same hours might be better spent talking with each other, playing with each other, reading, pursuing a hobby or some other creative endeavor, or learning a new skill. When we all complain we have so little time, why should we sacrifice so much of this precious commodity on the television god's altar?

84
Ask a trusted friend to help you gain perspective on your juggling routine.

We all have blind spots. We have lived our lives in the same way for so long that we can no longer perceive what we're doing right and what we're doing wrong. It's like seeing the back of your neck—you just can't do it.

That's why from time to time it's a good idea to do a reality check with a close friend. A friend can be more objective about our juggling habits; she will be able to tell us if we are juggling a realistic number of "balls"—or if it's time to consider setting some down. She may even be able to make suggestions that will help us juggle more efficiently.

There is no better looking glass
than an old friend.

THOMAS FULLER

*The heartfelt counsel of a friend is
as sweet as perfume and incense.*

PROVERBS 27:9 NLT

85
Avoid procrastination.

There are some jobs I tend to put off doing. The longer I put them off, the more I hate to even think about them. . . and the more I hate to think about them, the longer I put them off. Gradually, these tasks assume enormous, threatening proportions in my mind. They loom over my life, casting a shadow across my juggling routine. As I force myself to work around these dreaded jobs, they begin to actually cost me more effort and time than if I just did them and got them over with.

Remember when your mother used to tell you to eat the thing on your plate you liked least before you ate anything else? The same strategy applies to these unattractive activities we all put off doing. The best approach is simply to do them quickly and get them over—and then feel free to go on to the activities we truly enjoy.

*Procrastination is
the thief of time.*

EDWARD YOUNG

86
Let go of your need to be in a hurry.

We live in a rushed culture. In fact, we seem to feel that the faster the pace of our life, the more worthwhile we are as people. We hurry to cram as many accomplishments as we can into our limited twenty-four-hour days.

But the best things in life, the eternal things in life, can seldom be hurried. Things like relationships. . .and forgiveness and understanding . . .and creativity. . .and our souls. These things are like trees that grow so slowly and patiently we cannot see them moving.

If our priorities are worldly achievement and recognition, then we will continue to hurry—but if our mission in life is an eternal one, we will slow down enough to see the sure, sweet movement of God's grace in our lives.

Only by stepping back can we spot
. . .how addictive it is to be rushed and busy.
. . .Busyness can keep us from having to
reflect, risk intimacy, or face the void.
. . .We're never forced to ask ourselves
what really matters.

RALPH KEYES

Christ was never in a hurry.
There was no rushing forward,
no anticipating, no fretting
over what might be.
Each day's duties were done
as every day brought them,
and the rest was left with God.

MARY SLESSOR

87
Be a peak performer— not a workaholic.

Which one are you? Ernie J. Zelinski, in his book titled *The Joy of Not Working*, defines peak performers and workaholics this way:

A peak performer is someone who. . .

- works regular hours.
- has defined goals.
- delegates as much as possible.
- has many interests outside of work.
- takes and enjoys vacations.
- has deep friendships outside of work.
- minimizes conversation about work matters.
- can enjoy "goofing off."
- feels life is a celebration.

A workaholic, on the other hand, is someone who. . .

- works long hours.
- has no defined goals (works simply for the sake of working).
- cannot delegate work to others.
- has no interests outside of work.
- misses vacations to work.
- always talks about work matters.
- is always busy doing something.
- feels life is difficult.

In order to seek one's own direction, one must simplify the mechanics of ordinary, everyday life.

PLATO

88
Welcome each day
as a chance to begin again.

Once we drop a "ball" or break a resolution to do things in a new way, we sometimes give up altogether. *What's the point?* we tell ourselves. *I might as well just quit trying. I'll never be able to change.*

No, we probably won't ever change if we allow ourselves to become discouraged so easily. But we have another option. We can begin each morning with fresh resolution.

A new life begins for us each day. All we have to do is step forward and live it.

Every morning we have
twenty-four brand-new hours to live.

THICH NHAT HANH

*This is the day
the LORD has made;
let us rejoice and be glad in it.*

PSALM 118:24

Yesterday is gone.
Tomorrow is not yet come.
We have only today.
Let us begin.

MOTHER TERESA

89
Remember that sometimes less is really more.

Our world likes big. Big hamburgers. . .big bagels. . .big superstores. . .big homes. We are convinced that if some of something is good, then more of it will have to be better yet. We like to accumulate possessions; our goal is to have more.

What we don't realize, though, is that more of everything also means that whatever it is will take up more of our time. Think about it. The bigger the plate of food, the longer it takes you to eat it. The larger the store, the more time you will need to find what you need. And the more rooms your house has, the longer it will take you to keep them clean and picked up.

There's nothing wrong with having what we need, or enjoying the material blessings God has given us. But how much do we really need?

*Perhaps too much of everything is
as bad as too little.*

EDNA FERBER

～⟩⟩

Often people attempt to live their lives
backwards: they try to have more things,
or more money, in order to do more of what
they want so that they will be happier.
The way it actually works is the reverse.
You must first be who you really are,
then, do what you need to do,
in order to have what you want.

MARGARET YOUNG

90
Be optimistic.

Sometimes we forget that the apostle Paul included hope with faith and love when he spoke of the three things that will endure (1 Corinthians 13:13). We focus on faith and love, but hope seems less practical to us somehow, more vague and hazy. But I doubt Paul threw the word hope into his sentence just because he felt he needed an extra word to make the phrase sound better. I'm sure he knew what he was talking about.

Hope means we are confident that our future is in God's hands. Of course, all of us get discouraged sometimes. But an optimistic attitude will keep us pointed forward toward our vision. It will keep us looking toward what lies ahead, ready to take risks and bring about change. It will direct our sense of priorities and help us stay focused.

Despair and pessimism make the "balls" we

juggle seem heavy and awkward. Optimism, however, lightens our load.

*No pessimist ever discovered
the secret of the stars,
or sailed to an uncharted land,
or opened a new heaven
to the human spirit.*

HELEN KELLER

91
Live each day as though it were your last.

One good way to determine your priorities is to ask yourself this question: What would I do if today were the last day of my life? This question is not meant to give us a sense of dread or desperation; instead, it can help us see what things are necessary and vital in our lives—and which things are dead wood we would cut away in a second if we knew our time on earth was limited.

If today were our last, I suspect all of us would be more patient with the ones we love. We would make sure they knew how much we loved them. We would take time to appreciate the beauty and wonder of life. . .a sunrise, the sun shining through our kitchen windows, the feel of the wind on our faces, the sound of a bird singing in our backyard. We might think about what we could do with our last hours to build the kingdom of God. I'm sure we would talk often to God.

Why wait until it really is your last day on earth? Take advantage of the gift of time God has given you. Enjoy and use each moment with all your heart.

It's only when we truly know
and understand that we have
a limited time on earth—
and that we have no way of knowing
when our time is up—
that we will begin to
live each day to the fullest,
as if it was the only one we had.

ELIZABETH KUBLER-ROSS

92
Accept your life's circumstance.

We all have in our minds images of the way we want our lives to be. When life doesn't measure up to those images, instead of accepting whatever is, we tend to hold onto those imaginary pictures, refusing to let them go. This is the way things ought to be, we insist stubbornly. As we refuse to accept the reality of our lives, we become frustrated and angry and resentful.

I'm certain God doesn't want us to passively accept injustice and human cruelty. But we can choose to look at the small, ordinary circumstances of our lives as His presents to us. Instead of turning away in disappointment from these gifts, we can open our hearts and accept them. As Mary did when Gabriel came to tell her about Jesus' birth, we can choose to say "Yes" to whatever God sends us.

Our willingness to say yes transforms the reality of our lives. It allows the Spirit's presence

to infuse even the most humdrum events. We
will no longer waste our time and energy carrying a heavy load of resentment; instead, we will
find ourselves juggling our lives with God.

Our task is to say a holy yes to
the real things of our lives as they exist.

NATALIE GOLDBERG

⦚

*God give us the grace to accept with
serenity
the things that cannot be changed.*

REINHOLD NIEBUHR

⦚

I have learned to be content
whatever the circumstances.

THE APOSTLE PAUL (PHILIPPIANS 4:11)

93
*Don't wait until tomorrow
to begin living your life.*

I'll begin managing my time better. . .

- when I finish this project.
- when I feel better.
- when I get past this family crisis.
- when I get caught up with my bills.

When life gets back to normal, we tell our-selves, then I'll get my juggling routine worked out. When things are calm again, I'll start tak-ing time for God. . .I'll look at my priorities. . . I'll make time for myself. . .I'll change.

Face it, though—the way life is right now, well, this is normal. Life will always offer us one crisis after another to handle. We can't count on long calm stretches when we will have the time and leisure to learn new skills.

Besides, it's in the midst of the crisis that we

most need to learn better ways to juggle our lives.

Life never calms down
long enough for
us to wait until tomorrow
to start living the life we deserve.

SARAH BAN BREATHNACH

94
Establish household rules.

This book is about forming small new habits and attitudes that will help us manage our time better. If you can also teach both yourself and your family the following habits, you may find you have more time for the things your heart longs to do.

Consider establishing these four simple rules in your household:

- If you take it out, put it back.
- If you drop it, pick it up.
- If you open it, close it.
- If you take it off, hang it up.

Do not let trifles disturb
your tranquility of mind. . . .
Life is too precious to be sacrificed for the
nonessential and transient.

GRENVILLE KLEISER

95
Slow down.
Leave time in your life for "puttering."

Some days I reach the end of the workday with
a sense of accomplishment. I've checked off every
task on my to-do list; I've made significant
progress on some long-term goals; and I know
I've used every moment of my day efficiently and
productively. But other days, I look back and I
can't quite see what I did all day. I know I never
sat around watching the soaps and eating bon-
bons—and yet I just didn't seem to get all that
much done. Instead, I simply puttered around
my home and office, doing a little here and a little there, humming to myself, dreaming a little.

We need to stop feeling guilty for days like
that. We all need the refreshment and contentment they offer. They may even be what give us
the energy for the next high-power day when
we turn into superwomen.

And we are more apt to hear God's still, small

voice when we are quietly "puttering" than when we are steaming full-speed ahead.

*Puttering is really time to be alone,
to dream and to get
in touch with yourself.*

ALEXANDRA STODDARD

96
*Don't expect as much from
yourself during times of
emotional or physical trauma.*

If you are in the midst of a serious emotional
or physical crisis, you will need to set down
some of the "balls" you juggle. When you have
regained your strength, you can pick them up
again. But in the meantime, be gentle with
yourself. And know that God understands.

*As a father has compassion
on his children,
so the Lord has compassion
on those who fear him;
for he knows how we are formed.*

PSALM 103:13–14

97
Keep your eyes open for God's hand at work in your life.

We may become so preoccupied with our own efforts, so concentrated on the individual "balls" we are juggling, that we miss all the ways God is working in our lives. We assume we are doing everything with our own efforts—when all the while, He is working quietly and gently through the circumstances of our lives.

Become willing to see the hand of God and accept it as a friend's offer to help you with what you are doing.

JULIA CAMERON

98
Accept life's ups and downs.

Our minds can't help but absorb the ideas they are exposed to most often. When we feed our brains a steady diet of television philosophy, we find our expectations being shaped and molded by the artificial world we absorb each night. We become convinced that life should always be sunny and bright—and if we do encounter some small, mildly humorous problem, then a half hour is all it takes to resolve it. Watching commercials can be even worse for our thinking. We can't help but half believe in that pretend world where if we drink the right beverage, we will be ever young and joyful, and if we use the correct household cleaner, our homes will shine with serenity.

As silly as it seems, in my most desperate moments I've found myself longing to escape into soft drink commercials or being moved to tears by a commercial for cotton. I want that life. Why can't I find the same joy and peace in the reality of my own life? Why is my juggling routine so dismal?

Perhaps in a strange way television does offer us a glimpse of another reality, a reality that will one day be ours—not because we use a particular product, but because of Christ. In Eternity, we will be ageless and joyful and serene; time will have no more power to disturb us. If our hearts cry out for that reality, it's because that is our true home, the reality for which we were all created.

But in the meantime, in this world, we will always experience time's ups and downs. It doesn't mean we've done anything wrong. It's just the way life is. The up times may not last forever—but neither do the down times.

And God is with us as much in the down times as He is the up. His hand of blessing never stops touching our hearts.

*There are some things
you learn best in calm,
and some in storm.*

WILLA CATHER

99
Choose not to be a perfectionist.

Some of us are never happy unless things are absolutely perfect. We expect perfection from ourselves, from those around us, and from the circumstances of our lives.

Unfortunately, perfection is another one of those things we will never find in this world. Its home is in Eternity. Insisting on perfection here, within time's limitations, will only make us peevish, disapproving people, the sort of folk who experience no joy themselves and certainly give none to those around them.

Let go of your need for perfection. Relax. Accept yourself with all your imperfections. Accept the reality of those you love.

When you do, you'll find you juggle more lightly, more joyfully, and with less sense of tension and pressure.

*Perfectionism is
the voice of the oppressor,
the enemy of the people.
It will keep you cramped and insane
your whole life.*

ANNE LAMOTT

100
Leave room in your life for grace and wonder.

You can't schedule grace; you can't put a deadline on miracles. There's no way you can write on your daily planner between 2:00 and 3:00 P.M., "hour of grace," and then say to God, "I have an opening here for You. This would be a convenient time for You to bless me."

If we want to make room in our lives for the miracle of grace, we need to leave empty spaces in our weekly schedule, moments for simply being rather than doing. We are all so focused on producing, achieving, accomplishing—but sometimes we need to simply breathe. . .and see what God does next.

Grace fills empty spaces, but it can only
enter where there is a void to receive it,
and it is grace itself which makes this void.

SIMONE WEIL

*There are only two ways
to live your life.
One is as though
nothing is a miracle.
The other is as though
everything is a miracle.*

ALBERT EINSTEIN

101
Be confident that God loves you even in your most disorganized moments.

As you learn to juggle more smoothly, God will smile with you as you look at your ordered home and finished projects; He will rejoice as you work to accomplish your mission in His kingdom; and He will bless you as you make Him the focus of your daily routine.

But on those days—and we all have them—when everything falls apart, when you seem to accomplish nothing at all, and God seems far away, He is still with you. He may ache for your pain, but He still smiles when He looks at you; He still rejoices in your life; and He still longs to reach out and bless you.

Learning to use your time more efficiently will not make you any more valuable in God's eyes. It may make you a bit happier; you may feel a sense of fulfillment as you create a life where you have time for the things that matter most to you. But it will not make you more worthy of God's love.

Only Christ's grace does that.

Getting more done doesn't ensure that you will be happier; it just means you get more done.

LEE SILBER

≀≀

There is a time for everything, and a season for every activity under heaven.

ECCLESIASTES 3:1

$\mathcal{O}$ my God,
grant that I may so wait upon Thee,
that when quick decision and action
are needed I may mount up
with wings as an eagle;
and when under direction of Thy
will and the needs of the people
I have to keep going under pressure,
I may run and not be weary;
and in times of routine and humble duty,
I may walk and not faint.
For all my fresh springs are in Thee,
O God of my strength.

GEORGE APPLETON

Inspirational Library

Beautiful purse/pocket-size editions of Christian classics bound in flexible leatherette. These books make thoughtful gifts for everyone on your list, including yourself!

When I'm on My Knees   The highly popular collection of devotional thoughts on prayer, especially for women.
   Flexible Leatherette $4.97

The Bible Promise Book   Over 1,000 promises from God's Word arranged by topic. What does God promise about matters like: Anger, Illness, Jealousy, Love, Money, Old Age, and Mercy? Find out in this book!
   Flexible Leatherette $3.97

Daily Wisdom for Women   A daily devotional for women seeking biblical wisdom to apply to their lives. Scripture taken from the New American Standard Version of the Bible.
   Flexible Leatherette $4.97

My Daily Prayer Journal   Each page is dated and features a Scripture verse and ample room for you to record your thoughts, prayers, and praises. One page for each day of the year.
   Flexible Leatherette $4.97

Available wherever books are sold.
Or order from:

Barbour Publishing, Inc.
P.O. Box 719
Uhrichsville, OH 44683
http://www.barbourbooks.com

If you order by mail, add $2.00 to your order for shipping.
Prices are subject to change without notice.